Implementing EU Environmental Law in Italy

# Implementing EU Environmental Law in Italy

Giovanni Di Cosimo (Ed.)

eleven international publishing

*Published, sold and distributed by Eleven International Publishing*
P.O. Box 85576
2508 CG The Hague
The Netherlands
Tel.: +31 70 33 070 33
Fax: +31 70 33 070 30
e-mail: sales@budh.nl
www.elevenpub.com

*Sold and distributed in USA and Canada*
International Specialized Book Services
920 NE 58th Avenue, Suite 300
Portland, OR 97213-3786, USA
Tel: 1-800-944-6190 (toll-free)
Fax: +1-503-280-8832
orders@isbs.com
www.isbs.com

Eleven International Publishing is an imprint of Boom uitgevers Den Haag.

ISBN 978-94-6236-064-8
ISBN 978-94-6094-772-8 (E-book)



Printed in The Netherlands

# Table of Contents

**Introduction** 1

1 **EU Environmental Policy** 3
*Eugenia Bartoloni*

2 **Introduction to European Environmental Directives** 17
*Erik Longo*

3 **Mechanisms for Implementing EU Law at State Level** 23
*Pietro Falletta and Nicola Lupo*

4 **The Implementation of EU Law at Regional Level** 39
*Giovanni Di Cosimo*

5 **Infringement Proceedings** 47
*Michela Angeli and Paolo Palchetti*

6 **Court of Justice's Rulings Against Italy Relating to Infringements of EU Environmental Law** 59
*Andrea Guazzarotti*

7 **Non-Compliance with European Environmental Law: Evidence from Case Study** 71
*Erik Longo and Claudia Pennacchietti*

8 **Infringement Proceedings Between Law and Practice** 89
*Angela Cossiri*

# Introduction

*Implementation has a cost. But the cost of non-implementation is very often much higher*
*(Communication by EU Commission, 7 March 2012)*

In September 2011, the European Commission sent to Italy a letter of formal notice for the failure to construct an adequate and integrated network of waste processing plants in the Campania region.[1] The following November, the Commission sent a letter of formal notice owing to the incomplete transposition of the Directive on waste electrical and electronic equipment.

These are two well-known examples of Italy's non-compliance with EU environmental laws. As underlined by the Commission, in these cases, Member States are obliged to sustain costs which are higher than the cost of correct implementation. The Treaty on the Functioning of the European Union (TFEU) provides in fact a very articulated control mechanism, incentives and penalties agains non-compliant Member States. However, Italy seems incapable of complying with the EU environmental acquis. Frequently, the implementation process becomes jammed, and in the most serious cases this can involve onerous consequences for the Italian State.

Indeed, in Italy such a process is very complex due to the participation of both central and regional institutions and administrations. According to another hypothesis, ineffective implementaton of EU environmental law is due to the distance between the actual conditions of the country and the requirements of the EU environmental policy; *i.e.* the initial mismatch between the Italian and the EU requested environmental standards is structurally too large to be fulfilled within the timing established by the European institutions.

Whatever the cause, the high number of infringement procedures against Italy remains an indication of the difficulty the country has in transposing and applying the EU environmental acquis.

This volume reviews the phenomenon of the difficult implementation of EU environmental law in Italy in order to highlight not only the causes, but the forms of manifestation.[2]

The analysis is conducted through different steps. The first part considers the EU environmental acquis and documents which of the legislative acts result the most difficult to implement (Chapters 1 and 2). The second part examines the tools foreseen in the Italian

1 The procedure ex Art. 260 TFEU was launched following Italy's lasting failure to comply after a first ruling of the ECJ rendered under Art. 258 TFEU in March of the same year, C-297/08, *Commission v. Italy* [2010] ECR I-1749.

2 The book is the result of the work by a group of researchers from the University of Macerata as part of the national project "The implementation of European Environmental Law" (Prin 2008), coordinated by Professor Caretti, University of Florence.

legal order to implement EU law both at central and regional levels (Chapters 3 and 4). In the third part the legal framework on infringement proceedings is explained (Chapter 5) in view of analyzing the Court of Justice's rulings against Italy in the sector (Chapter 6). The last part discusses some practical examples of non-compliance and describes how infringement cases are handled by the competent central administrations (Chapters 7 and 8).

# 1 EU Environmental Policy

*Eugenia Bartoloni*

## 1.1 Premise

As is well known, the process of European integration was set up with the intention, within the territory of the six founding States, of creating a common market based on the free circulation of persons, goods, services and capital, and characterized by competitive economical conditions which were neither disloyal nor falsified by interference from public administrative entities. Therefore, it may not be surprising that the treaty set out by the then European Economic Community (EEC), established around economical-commercial aims, did not foresee any form of discipline on environmental matters; neither is it by chance that the environmental policy became one of the priorities of community actions when its correlation with the need to regulate the market became evident. In the absence of an explicit legal basis which allows the European Union (EU) to adopt provisions in environmental matters, Union interventions were first based on Articles 115 TFEU (ex Art. 94 TEC)[1] and 352 TFEU (ex Art. 308 TEC).[2]

The measures based on the first provision, which introduces the harmonised legal framework, were required to complete the internal market, and especially to protect intra-community trade and avoid rules of unfair competition. The interventions based on the second provision, which provides for and disciplines the flexibility clause, were, on the other hand, inspired by the intention to fulfil the objectives indicated in the rather general terms pursuant to ex Article 2 TEC. Although for their diversity, both provisions enabled the EU to extend its range of action, allowing the institutions to act in a field such as that of environmental protection, which was not yet the object of a specific attribution of competence.

1 Art. 115 TFEU states: "Without prejudice to Article 114, the Council shall, acting unanimously in accordance with a special legislative procedure and after consulting the European Parliament and the Economic and Social Committee, issue directives for the approximation of such laws, regulations or administrative provisions of the Member States as directly affect the establishment or functioning of the internal market."

2 Art. 352 states: "1. If action by the Union should prove necessary, within the framework of the policies defined in the Treaties, to attain one of the objectives set out in the Treaties, and the Treaties have not provided the necessary powers, the Council, acting unanimously on a proposal from the Commission and after obtaining the consent of the European Parliament, shall adopt the appropriate measures. Where the measures in question area adopted by the Council in accordance with a special legislative procedure, it shall also act unanimously on a proposal from the Commission and after obtaining the consent of the European Parliament […]."

Only subsequently did the environmental field receive an explicit mention within the EC Treaty. At first, the Single European Act, which by in part codifying and systemising elements which resulted from a preceding practice, attributed an *ad hoc* basis to community intervention in environmental matters. Subsequently, the Maastricht Treaty not only did insert the objective of "sustainable development of Europe based on [...] a high level of protection and improvement of the quality of the environment" among the general aims of community action (now Art. 3, para. 3 TFEU), but it also transformed intervention in environmental matters into "policy" (now Title XX TFEU). More recently, the Treaty of Lisbon, in identifying a series of objectives in accordance with the TEU which are to inspire and guide the EU's general external action, inserted among others, the objective to "help develop international measures to preserve and improve the quality of the environment and the sustainable management of global natural resources, in order to ensure its sustainable development".[3]
In indicating that the objective of environmental protection must inspire every important action outside the EU, the latter provision strengthens and extends its range of action. Given the complexity and at the same time the specificity of the matter, the present analysis will limit itself to a review of the most relevant profiles of EU environmental law conducted on the model of the EU Treaty provisions (TEU and TFEU) and in the light of the most recent case law of the Court of Justice.

## 1.2 Objectives, Principles and Guidelines of the Environmental Policy

Article 191 TFEU, a provision which opens Title XX of the Treaty on Functioning of European Union dedicated to the environment, indicates, on one hand, the objectives connected with environmental policy (para. 1) and, on the other, the principles (para. 2) and the guidelines (para. 3) on which the EU actions undertaken on this competence are based. On recognizing the *ample discretionary power* of the EU legislator with regard to the implementation and the reciprocal reconciliation of the various objectives and principles contained in Article 191 TFEU, the European Court of Justice (ECJ) has constantly emphasized that judicial control on the institutional activity must be limited in principle to the manifest error of judgement. As the Court ruled

> in view of the need to strike a balance between certain objectives and principles mentioned in Article [191] and of the complexity of the implementation of those criteria, review by the Court must necessarily be limited to the question whether the Council, by adopting the Regulation, committed a manifest error of appraisal regarding the conditions for the application of Article [191] of the Treaty.[4]

3 Art. 21(2)(f) TEU.
4 Case C-284/95, *Safety Hi-Tech v. S. & T. Ltd.* [1998] ECR I-4301, para. 37; see also Case C-86/03, *Greek Republic v. Commission* [2005] ECR I-10979, para. 88.

### 1.2.1 Objectives

With reference to the objectives, paragraph 1 lists a series of aims, among which the objective of "protecting and improving the quality of the environment" assumes particular relevance. It deals with an ample and general definition which should justify interventions of environmental protection of various natures, levels and seriousness. From this point of view, the activities aimed at protecting, preserving and improving environmental quality should be based on Articles 191 *et seq.*, regardless of their general or specific, direct or indirect peculiarities which differ from case to case.

Also the other aims listed in paragraph 1 are not void of a general nature. The second of these concerns "protecting public health". While strengthening the conception of the environment as an asset involving interests of a non-exclusively environmental nature, it clearly indicates that measures predetermined to safeguard public health can also be included in the ambit of the application of Articles 191 *et seq.*[5] Furthermore, measures to safeguard public health could also be based on a multiplicity of legal bases considering that the institutions are obliged to guarantee an elevated level of public health protection in the definition and the transposition of all the EU policies and activities.[6]

The third objective, which concerns the "prudent and rational utilization of natural resources", indicates that environmental protection cannot exist without a prudent and attentive use of its resources. Although the notion of natural resource is not specified, it can easily be placed within the definition of assets – such as water, air, soil, fauna and flora, and particular natural ecosystems – which could be subject to deterioration or to depletion.[7] In this sense, the notion of an attentive and rational use of natural resources presents a certain contiguity with the concept of *sustainable development* to be found in several of the treaty's provisions.[8] Where the latter do not provide a definition, sustainable development can be intended as an objective it aims at the constant improvement of the quality of life on earth of both current and future generations and consists in safeguarding the earth's capacity to support life in all its diversity.[9] In this sense, the achievement of a sustainable development, which takes into consideration not only the current economical and

---

5 Recently, see Case C-28/08, *Commission v. Austria* [2011] ECR not yet published, para. 122.

6 See Art. 168 TFEU; see also Cases C-14/06, *European Parliament v. Commission* and C-295/06, *Kingdom of Denmark v. Commission* [2008] ECR I-1649, para. 75.

7 See Art. 2(12) Directive 2004/35/EC of the European Parliament and Council, 21st April 2004, on environmental responsibility on the issue of prevention and reparation of environmental damage, in OJ L 143, 30 April 2004, pp. 56 *et seq.*

8 See Art. 3(3), (5) TEU; Art. 21(2)(d), (f) TUE; Art. 11 TFEU.

9 Declaration on guiding principles for sustainable development, adopted by the European Council in Brussels, June 2005.

environmental interests but also those of future generations, cannot disregard an attentive use of natural resources.[10]

The last objective concerns "*promoting measures at international level to deal with regional or worldwide environmental problems* and, more specifically, to fighting climate changes". The provision clearly shows the EU vocation for intervening in the protection of environmental assets of a transnational or global nature, which are located wholly or partly outside their own Member State and situated in areas belonging to the sovereignty of other States or which are even not subject to national sovereignty. An example is the reference to climate change, which can be effectively contrasted only through interventions promoted on an international level.

Consistently with the objectives proclaimed in such ample terms, also the ECJ has given an extensive interpretation of the notion of environmental policy, more precisely defined as a policy which "seeks to [...] prevent, mitigate or eliminate the harmful effects of human activities on flora and fauna, soil, water, air, climate, landscape and sites of particular interest, and on the health and quality of life of persons".[11] The general peculiarity which distinguishes EU objectives in environmental matters[12] has induced the Court to attribute the community legislator with an ample measure of discretionality due to the nature and extent of the measures to be adopted.[13] Only the obviously inappropriate nature of such measures with regard to the scope pursued could undermine its legitimacy. In fact, *consistently with the principle of proportionality*, the chosen methods cannot exceed what is strictly necessary to achieve the objectives of environmental protection, becoming useless interventions which are damaging to the other rights or freedoms guaranteed in accordance with the treaties.[14] Under this profile, therefore, the Court, while attributing the maximum priority to the objectives of environmental protection, has recognized the need to balance with *other equally fundamental interests* for Union law.

10 Only in this limited exception, sustainable development seems to present a determinable content. Otherwise, the notion, intending more ample terms as a general necessity to not compromise the capacity of future generations to satisfy their needs, would seem to have a content which is judicially vague, unsuitable to function as a guideline to assess the legitimacy of the derived legal provisions.

11 Case C-280/02, *Commission v. French Republic* [2004] ECR I-8573, para. 15.

12 Case C-379/92 *Peralta* [1994] ECR I-3453, para. 57; Case C-284/95, *Safety Hi-Tech* [1998] ECR, para. 43. Recently, Case C-378/08, *Raffinerie Mediterranee (ERG) Spa et al. v. Ministero dello sviluppo economico et al.* [2010] ECR I-1919, para. 45; Joint Cases C-379/08, *Raffinerie Mediterranee (ERG) Spa et al. v. Ministero dello sviluppo economico et al.* and C-380/09, *ENI Spa v. Ministero Ambiente e Tutela del Territorio e del Mare et al.* [2010] ECR I-2007, para. 38.

13 Case C-343/09 *Afton Chemical Limited* [2010] ECR paras. 28 and 33.

14 See Joint Cases C-260/06 and 261/06, *Escalier et al.* [2007] ECR I-9717, para. 37.

### 1.2.2 The Principles

Paragraph 2 of Article 191 TFEU establishes that

> EU policy on the environment shall aim at a high level of protection taking into account the diversity of situations in the various regions of the European Union. It shall be based on the precautionary principle and on the principle that preventive action should be taken, that environmental damage should as a priority be rectified at source and that the polluter shall pay.

The provision in question indicates, therefore, the general principles on which the EU measures on environmental matters must be based.

Among these, *the high level of protection*, which constitutes the qualitative guideline to which the EU interventions on environmental matters must aspire, is surely the most transversal principle among those identified under Article 191.[15] Although the treaties do not provide a definition, the fact that it may justify the adoption of measures equalized on the lowest common environmental denominator shared by the other States must be excluded. In a similar way, the opposite interpretation seems to be excluded: the principle in question should not require the highest form of protection among those technically accessible.[16] Instead, the call for a situation of diversity in the various regions of the EU when it is deemed necessary to determine what could be considered a high degree of protection in the specific case, seems to suggest that this principle is aimed at allowing those more "backward" regions, under the profile of protection, to align themselves with the standards of the more "advanced" regions. In practice, the principle of the high degree of protection is constantly used by the Court as a guideline to interpret technical notions,[17] or to establish the existence or not of conditions of exemption to specific bans.[18]

The *principle of precaution* justifies the adoption of protective measures, potentially damaging to the other's interest, when, despite the absence of specific scientific findings, there is the risk that assets of an environmental type, or even public health, may be compromised. According to the Court "where there is uncertainty as to the existence or extent

15 It is also pursuant to Art. 3(3) TEU; Art. 114(3) TFEU; Art. 168(1) TFEU.

16 See the most recent ruling, Case C-77/09, *Gowan Comércio Internacional e Serviços Lda v. Ministero della Salute* [2010] ECR not yet published, para. 73.

17 Joint Cases C-175/98 and C-177/98, *Lirussi e Bizzaro* [1999] ECR I-6881, para. 5; Case C-387/97, *Commission v. Greece* [2000] ECR I-5047, para. 94.

18 Directive 2006/12/EC of the European Parliament and Council, 5 April 2006, relative to waste, in OJ L 114, 27 April 2006, pp. 9 *et seq*.

of risks to the health of consumers", the principle of precaution allows the institutions to adopt "protective measures without having to wait until the reality and the seriousness of those risks become fully apparent"[19] or that the negative effects on public health take concrete form. The application of the principle therefore, concerns the management of the risk of a threat for the protection of environmental interests in all those situations in which its complete assessment may be hindered by the precariousness or insufficiency of scientific data.

Additional to the principle of precaution is the one of *preventive action* "by virtue of (that) it is for the Community and the Member States to prevent, reduce, and, in so far as is possible, eliminate from the outset, the sources of pollution or nuisance by adopting measures of a nature such as to eliminate recognized risks".[20] The principle of prevention therefore, induces the legislator to act preventively in order to avoid at the onset risks of prejudice for the environment and public health, rather than intervene subsequently to make amends. Furthermore, seeing as it presupposes the existence of known risks, on the contrary to that of precaution, it is based on a certain degree of certainty with regard to scientific data. Although the principles of precaution and prevention have different ambits of application, in judicial practice they are often evoked jointly.

The *principle of correction at source* has, differently from those just mentioned, a restorative, compensatory and sanctioning function; it presupposes in other words, that the damage has been proved. On requiring the reparatory action to be performed as near as possible to the source once the damage has been determined, the principle in question is preordained to contain the damaging effects to the environment deriving from the event as much as possible. With the adoption of Directive 2006/12/EC,[21] the principle of correction has found ample application in the matter of waste disposal. It indicates that

> it is for each region, municipality or other local authority to take appropriate steps to ensure that its own waste is collected, treated and disposed of and that that waste must accordingly be disposed of as close as possible to the place where it is produced, in order to limit as far as possible the transportation of waste.[22]

The principle of "the polluter pays", which completes the system of the general principles, has both a preventive and a reparatory function. In other words, it is inspired not only by the need to oblige industries to sustain the environmental costs deriving from their

19 Case C-297/08, *Commission v. Italy* [2010] ECR I-1749, para. 67.

20 Joint Cases C-175/98 and C-177/98, *Lirussi e Bizzaro* [1999] ECR I-6881, para. 51; Case C-387/97, *Commission v. Greece* [2000] ECR I-5047, para. 94.

21 Directive 2006/12/EC of the European Parliament and Council, 5 April 2006, relative to waste, in OJ L 114, 27 April 2006, pp. 9 *et seq.*

22 Case C-297/08, *Commission v. Italy* [2010] ECR I-1749, para. 67.

activities but also from the need to charge them with the reparation costs for the environmental damage caused during these activities. Therefore, it is with reference to such situations that the institutions have foreseen under Directive 2004/35/EC,[23] a system of civil responsibility suitable to allow the payment of penalties for damage to the environment. This Directive, which was issued in order to establish a common discipline for the prevention and reparation of damage, sets a detailed framework of responsibility based on the principle of "the polluter pays", according to which the subject who caused the environmental damage, or an imminent risk of such damage, is financially responsible.

The Court has constantly upheld that the principles on which EU environmental policy is based, similarly to the objectives that inspired the action, are addressed to the EU legislator. On the basis of this premise, it has reached the conclusion that, in the absence of a provision at European level, it cannot be invoked by physical or judicial entities. For the Court

> since Article [191 TFEU], is directed at action [at Community level], that provision cannot be relied on as such by individuals in order to exclude the application of national legislation [...] in an area covered by environmental policy for which there is no Community legislation adopted on the basis of Article [192 TFEU], that specifically covers the situation in question.[24]

Whenever the Court does not provide further indications, it is reasonable to think that the unsuitability of the principles and the objectives to be invoked directly by private entities attains to their *unsuitability to produce direct effects*.[25]

### 1.2.3 *The Guidelines*

Lastly, while planning environmental policy, pursuant to paragraph 3, Article 191, TFEU, EU institutions must take some guidelines into consideration. Among these, the most incisive guideline is that which refers to "available scientific and technical data".[26] This refers to a parameter which expresses the need for an environmental

23 Directive 2004/35/EC of the European Parliament and Council, 21 April 2004, on the environmental liability with regard to the prevention and remedying of environmental damage, in OJ L 143, 30 April 2004, pp. 56 *et seq.*

24 Case C-378/08, *Raffinerie Mediterranee (ERG) Spa et al. v. Ministry for the Development of Economy et al.* [2010] para. 46.

25 The direct effect is the suitability of a provision, formulated as a guideline for Member States or for institutions, to create rights and obligations in the hands of individuals and legal entities which can be invoked before a National judge .The Court has constantly highlighted that a provision is suitable to produce direct effects when it presents certain requisites: it is clear, precise and of an unconditional nature.

26 Case C-343/09, *Afton Chemical Limited* [2010], para. 32; Case C-405/07 P, *Holland v. Commission* [2008] ECR I-8301, para. 61.

policy which is constantly updated to techno-scientific progress and which is consistent with its interventions. The other guidelines which refer respectively to "environmental conditions in the various regions of the Union" and to the "potential benefits" and "costs of action or lack of action" to the "economic and social development of the Union as a whole and the balanced development of its regions", are not explicitly mentioned in Court case law. However, this does not exclude that at the moment in which an institution deliberates a measure on environmental matters it should "take account of all the relevant evidence and explain, in its final decision, the essential considerations which led it to adopt that decision".[27] Consequently, non-compliance with the obligations set in paragraph 3 of Article 191 TFEU for the competent institution means, ultimately, the violation of the *obligation to state reasons*.

### 1.3 The Nature of Competence

On the basis of attribution set out in the treaties, competences attributed to the EU can be distinguished as being exclusive, shared and coordinative. Environmental matters as explicitly established by Article 4, paragraph 2, TFEU, belong to the ambit of *shared competences*. This means that both the EU and the Member States are at the same time detainers of the power to adopt provisions. To establish to whom the exercise of competence pertains in the concrete case, the *principle of subsidiarity* states that

> if and insofar as the objectives of the proposed action cannot be sufficiently achieved by Member States, either at central level or regional and local level, but can rather, by reason of the scale or effects of the proposed action, be better achieved at Union level.[28]

Once the EU has exercised its competence, the adopted discipline excludes any whatsoever legislative divergence of any other Member States, unless this is explicitly authorized by the same EU provisions. This for instance, is exactly the case of the directives concerning environmental matters. In the presence of directives of harmonization which, while indicating the minimum standards for environmental protection, leaves Member States the faculty to adopt stricter rules, the States will be held to respect the minimum requirements, but may also set *higher levels of protection*. The Court has in fact ruled that "the protective measures adopted pursuant to Article [192] are not to

27 Case C-405/07 P, para. 67.
28 Art. 5(3) TEU.

prevent any Member State from maintaining or introducing more stringent protective measures compatible with the Treaty".[29] This faculty has been generalized by Article 193 TFEU, which in fact, foresees the possibility for Member States to derogate to EU discipline with an aim of guaranteeing "more stringent protective measures".[30]

However, determining the nature of EU competence to *conclude international agreements* on environmental matters is much more complicated. Article 191, paragraph 4, TFEU determines that "within their respective spheres of competence, the Union and Member States shall cooperate with third countries and with the competent international organizations. The arrangements for Union cooperation may be the subject of agreements between the Union and the third parties concerned. The previous subparagraph shall be without prejudice to Member States competence to negotiate in international bodies and to conclude international agreements." From this provision, it could be deduced that the competence to conclude agreements on environmental cooperation throughout the entire range of the EU environmental competence was shared between the EU and the Member States. However, this does not prevent the EU from concluding agreements going further than the mere cooperation. In this case, however, the agreement may not be based on Article 191, paragraph 4, TFEU;[31] rather EU competence will find its justification, if it is the case, on the basis of the *principle of parallelism* of internal and external competences. This principle of judicial origin,[32] establishes the existence of EU competence to conclude agreements in parallel with that which it has already exercised to adopt legislative acts. More precisely, the EU detains an exclusive power to conclude agreements productive of obligations, the implementation of which involves an interference with pre-existing internal law.[33] Therefore, the competence to stipulate agreements, results as not derived from a treaty rule which explicitly confers relative power to the EU, but rather, implicitly, from the previous adoption of internal legislation which could be prejudiced by the conventional obligations. The principle responds to a double ratio: on one hand it allows the EU to integrate internal legislation with agreements, also when this is not foreseen by the

29 Case C-379/92, *Peralta* [1994], para. 57.

30 See Section 1.6.

31 Opinion 2/00, protocol of *Cartagena to the Convention on the biological diversity* [2001] ECR I-9713, para. 43.

32 The principle of parallelism was established for the first time in the AETS ruling (Case 22/70, *Commissione v. Consiglio* [1971] ECR, p. 263).

33 In the sentence AETS the court judgment was as follows: "Whenever (with a view to implementing a common policy envisaged by the Treaty) the Community adopts provisions laying down common rules, whatever form these may take, the Member States no longer have the right, acting individually or even collectively, to undertake obligations with third countries which affect those rules. As these common provisions are gradually adopted, in fact, the competence to transpose and to fulfil the obligations towards other States is centred in the Community-with effect for the entire sphere in which the community provision is in force" (para. 17).

treaty; on the other, it prevents Member States, through international agreements, from concluding obligations capable of affecting that legislation.

Although the case law may not always be linear[34] on environmental matters, the Court seems to admit the coexistence of two categories of such relevant external powers which are so different: that conferred by Article 191, paragraph 4, TFEU and that deriving from the principle of parallelism.[35] While the first does not exclude a concomitant power of the States to conclude agreements, the adoption of internal legislation prevents Member States from undertaking commitments which could interfere with such provisions. With regard to their extent, while Article 191 limits itself to exclusively disciplining forms of cooperation, the principle of parallelism gives the EU the competence to conclude agreements on all environmental matters but only in the measure with which the agreement terms affect internal legislation.

In practice, faced with the variety of the material sectors touched by the multilateral agreements concerning environmental matters, these are generally concluded in a mixed form, that is at the same time by the EU and the Member States on one side and by third States on the other. This modality, in fact, allows an undertaking of commitments which, by relevance or by objective, could not wholly be charged to the competence of the EU, nor to that of the Member States.

## 1.4 THE LEGAL BASES

Articles 191 TFEU *et seq.* are not the only provisions on which the EU policy on environmental matters is based.

First of all, because environmental protection is conceived by the treaty on the Functioning as a suitable *transversal policy*, and as such integrated into the ambit of the other EU policies and actions.[36] Consequently, the EU legislator may decide to promote environmental protection, constantly defined as one of the essential objectives of the EU, also in the ambit of the actions undertaken on the basis of other competences.[37]

34 In some recent rulings, the Court seemed to mitigate the traditional requisites identified in the AETS sentence, that is to say the existence of common rules on which the agreement is influenced. It would seem to be sufficient to base EU competence to stipulate the agreement on environmental matters which the deriving obligations affect "a field in large measure covered", when they are not the object of a specific discipline (Case C-240/09, *Lesoochranárske zoskupenie VLK v. Ministerstvo životného prostredia Slovenskej republiky (Convenzione di Aarhus)* [2011] ECR not yet published, paras 36 *et seq.*; Case C-459/03, *Commission v. Irelanda (Mox Plant)* [2006] ECR I-4635, para. 95; Case C-239/03, *Commission v. Francia* [2004] ECR I-9325, para. 30).

35 Cannizzaro, 2007.

36 See Art. 11 TFEU pursuant to which "[The] environmental protection requirements must be integrated into the definition and implementation of the Union policies and activities..." and to Art. 21(2)(d) TFEU which sanctions the integration of environmental policy in the ambit of the policy of development cooperation.

37 Case C-440/05, *Commission v. Council* [2007] ECR I-9097, para. 60; Case C-28/09, *Commission v. Austria* [2011] ECR not yet reported, para. 121.

Second, because the treaty explicitly foresees the *concurrence of other legal bases* on the basis of which measures can be adopted which, while intended for the completion of the internal market, are also provided with an environmental aim.[38] Finally, because many acts present a *complex content*, which is not immediately linked to the exercise of one competence rather than another. The numerous unilateral agreements stipulated by the EU are an example of this, which, on disciplining the crossborder movements of refuse, of dangerous substances or of genetically modified organisms, are suitable, both for object and finality, to fall within common commercial policy as in the environmental policy.

If, therefore, measures of an environmental type can be undertaken also on the legal bases different from those foreseen under Articles 191 TFEU *et seq.*, it becomes essential to establish the correct legal basis of an act which, in addition to the environmental aim, also touches other material profiles. In fact, when determining the proceedings to follow, the legal basis reflects the role reserved to each institution in the ambit of each decisional procedure.

Therefore, whenever the treaty provisions on which actions could be based concerning environmental matters are potentially numerous, the Court has determined that the choice of the legal bases must be carried out in *objective terms*, specifying with this aim the scope and principal content of the act.[39] As so defined by the Court, the test, which establishes a reasonable connection between the essential or peculiar content of an act and a legal basis, has been elaborated in order to avoid the accumulation of legal bases when the act, further to its particular objective, consists of provisions of an accessory type which recall other legal bases.[40] The accumulation of legal bases is, in fact, a rather complex operation, and not infrequently capable of altering the institutional equilibrium of the treaty. Only in the presence of an Act which pursues more inseparably connected principal aims would the possibility to use the corresponding different legal bases contemporaneously be exceptionally allowed.[41] Even though this solution is aimed at preventing essential aspects of the Act from being adopted according to a procedure different from that provided for in the treaties, the Court has excluded the *accumulation of legal bases*, in the event that the utilization of more legal bases rather than guarantee the institutional dynamics should have the effect of altering the equilibriums.[42]

---

38 It refers to Arts. 114 and 115 TFEU V., para. 1.

39 See, among the first, Case C-300/89, *Commission v. Council* [1991] ECR, p. I-2867.

40 See opinion 2/00, paras 22 *et seq.*

41 *Ibid.*, para. 23.

42 See among others, Case C-300/89 [1991]. According to the Court, whenever the competence of an institution is based on two Treaty provisions, the institution must adopt the acts corresponding to the guidelines for both the provisions under considerations. It has however excluded the accumulation of legal guidelines in the cases in which together with a diversity of a judicial base there is a diversity in the proceedings for which the procedure most guaranteed and most respectful of the democratic principle is likely to divest the cooperation procedure of its very substance (see para. 18 of the sentence).

## 1.5 THE FINANCING AND EXECUTION OF EU PROVISIONS

In the face of the execution of the legislative power of the EU, it is the responsibility of the Member States, except for some technical implementation provisions, to provide for the financing and execution of environmental policy. This is set down in Article 192, paragraph 4, TFEU, which, compliant with the principles of indirect administration and subsidiarity, indicates that Member States are responsible for the financing and implementation of measures deliberated on a European level. In reaffirming these principles, the Court has admitted that

> a Member State may not plead practical or administrative difficulties in order to justify non-compliance with the obligations and time-limits laid down in Community directives. The same holds true of financial difficulties, which it is for the Member States to overcome by adopting appropriate measures.[43]

Only in the case whereby a measure implicates such disproportionate costs for the public authorities of a Member State does paragraph 5 of Article 192 foresee that the institutions must contextually concede temporary derogations and, additionally or alternatively, financial contributions through the cohesion fund. These exceptions, still pursuant to paragraph 5 of Article 192 are not applied where the excessive costs concern the implementation of the principle "the polluter pays", which, as is known, is aimed at making the financial operators sustain the costs of environmental protection with which they could be charged.

## 1.6 CONCLUSIONS

In conclusion to the limited review performed in the previous paragraphs, it would be worthwhile to focus our attention on two specific aspects destined to have a pronounced impact on the ambit of national legal procedures.

It has been observed above all, that environmental policy is "transversal". This means that the EU institutions are obliged to ensure an adequate protection of the environment, not only in the elaboration of the specific territorial aspect, but also in the pursuit of the other EU actions and policies. The transversal aspect of environmental policy means, consequently, that the States must comply with the environmental standards determined by the EU, not only when they are called to apply the specific sector legislation, but also when they are obliged to implement the provisions which are set in the implementation ambit of other actions and policies. In principle, therefore, any infringements by Member States

43 Case C-42/89, *Commission v. Belgium* [1990] I-2821, para. 24.

in environmental matters can originate, not only from the failure to implement or the inexact implementation of directives based on the specific sector guidelines, but also from violations of standards foreseen by non-"environmental" provisions (*e.g.* in the field of energy, transport, etc.)
Under a different profile, through an event characterized by a strong institutional contrast concerning the identification of the correct legal basis, the competence of the EU to adopt, pursuant to Article 192, environmental measures of a penal aspect has been confirmed. Significant to this end is the adoption of Directive 2008/99/EC, which introduces a minimum standard on the elements relative to environmental violations to the legislation of the Member State.[44] It is therefore easy to understand how, on the evolution aspect of the relationship between Member State criminal law and Union law, this Directive carries a certain weight: it represents the first complete manifestation of sopranational intervention aimed at harmonizing the Criminal systems of Member States in order to guarantee effectiveness in environmental protection. The Treaty of Lisbon should further contribute to this harmonization process having foreseen in Article 83 paragraph 2, TFEU the competence of the EU to set down minimum legal requirements relating not only to the definition of crimes but also of sanctions when this is "essential to ensure the effective implementation of a Union policy in an area which has been subject to harmonization measures". It does not seem hazardous to hypothesize that, through this latter provision, EU environmental legislation is destined to exercise an even more widespread influence in the ambit of national legal systems.

## REFERENCES

S. Amadeo, 'Articoli 174-176', *in* A. Tizzano (a cura di), *Trattati dell'Unione europea e della Comunità europea*, Milano, 2004, pp. 871 *et seq.*

E. Cannizzaro, 'Le relazioni esterne della Comunità verso un nuovo paradigma unitario?', *in Il Diritto dell'Unione europea*, 2007, pp. 223 *et seq.*

M. Clement, *Droit européen de l'environnement: jurisprudence commentée*, Bruxelles, 2010.

M.G. Faure, 'Effective, Proportional and Dissuasive Penalties in the Implementation of the Environmental Crime and Ship-source Pollution Directives: Questions and Challenges', *European Energy and Environmental Law Review*, 2010, pp. 256 *et seq.*

44 Directive 2008/99/EC of the European Parliament and Council, 19 November 2008 on the protection of the environment through criminal law in OJ 328, 6 December 2008, p. 28.

P. Fois, 'Il diritto ambientale nell'ordinamento dell'Unione Europea', *in* G. Cordini, P. Fois & S. Marchisio, *Diritto ambientale: profili internazionali europei e comparati*, Torino, 2008, pp. 51 *et seq.*

E. Herlin-Karnell, 'Commission v. Council: Some Reflections on Criminal Law in the First Pillar', *in European Public Law*, 2007, pp. 69 *et seq.*

J.H. Jans & H. Vedder, *European Environmental law* (3rd edn), Groningen, 2008.

L. Krämer, *EU Environmental Law* (7th edn), London, 2011.

M. Montint, 'EC External Relations on Environmental Law', *in* J. Scott (Ed.), *Environmental Protection: European Law and Governance*, Oxford, 2009, pp. 127 *et seq.*

G.M. Vagliasindi, 'La direttiva 2008/99/CE e il Trattato di Lisbona: verso un nuovo volto del diritto penale ambientale italiano', *in Diritto del commercio internazionale*, 2010, pp. 449 *et seq.*

P. Wennerås, 'Towards an Ever Greener Union? Competence in the Field of the Environment and Beyond', *Common Market Law Review*, 2008, pp. 1663 *et seq.*

# 2 Introduction to European Environmental Directives

*Erik Longo*

## 2.1 Introduction

The main purpose served by this chapter is to identify and give a concise explanation of the most important environmental directives that Italy has failed to transpose into national legislation. This brief presentation focuses on four sectors: biodiversity and nature conservation, water pollution, air protection, waste. At the end of the chapter, I will analyze other so-called "horizontal" directives for the lack of reference to one specific sector. Articles 3 TEU and 191(1) TFEU leave hardly any area of environmental policy outside the authority of the European Union (EU). These two articles refer to the environmental policy as a whole, not to the individual measure adopted under that policy. Although measures to realize the objectives of the Union's environmental policy may be based on any relevant article of the FEU Treaty, Articles 191 and 192 remain the most relevant provisions for EU environmental action.

The EU has adopted an important number of pieces of environmental legislation in the form of Regulations, Directives and non-binding Recommendations. The Union's environmental *acquis communautaire* comprises over 200 major legal acts covering a comprehensive array of environmental issues. Directives are the most frequently used instruments in EU environmental legislation. Usually a degree of detail provided for in a directive is less determined by the concept of "direct" than by the need to attain the different objective pursued. Detailed directives are frequent for areas of products, but are mostly used in sectors such as agriculture. In contrast, environmental directives tend to be of a more general nature. In particular, the debate over the last twenty-five years on subsidiarity and deregulation and the general loss of integration capacity of the EU has led to environmental directives which limit themselves to outlining general rules, framework provisions and basic requirements. Nevertheless, even environmental directives have, in recent years, had a tendency to force Member States to act in a certain way. Whether a directive cannot impose obligations on private persons, undertaking and associations, they can acquire rights from a directive in those cases where a provision is sufficiently concrete, precise and unconditional.

Member States have the duty to transpose directives in the national legal sysem, adopt the necessary implementing regulations and administrative rules, organize the relevant administrative agencies and enforce them in case of non-compliance.

It is well-established that those provisions of the directives that have been transposed into national law must actually be applied. This follows from the nature of the directive, which obliges Member States to achieve certain aims. It is not enough to take all practical steps to reach the directive's objectives. States must also achieve the directive's aims; directives do not leave it to the States' discretion as to whether they achieve the results or not.

### 2.2 Biodiversity and Nature Conservation

Nature conservation measures were among the first rules on environment the European Community adopted. Despite Member State reluctance to give this competence to the European Community, they favoured the negotiation and conclusion of international conventions devoted to the protection of nature or of part of it.[1] In this area the most important directive was adopted for the conservation of wild birds and the protection of the Habitat.

In 1979, the Community adopted Directive 79/409/EEC on the conservation of wild birds, following considerable public pressure in favour of such a measure. The Directive was reformed by Directive 2009/147/EU. This directive aimed at a comprehensive protection of all wild birds within the EU and outlined detailed provisions, in particular on hunting, capturing and trading of birds. Member States were asked to take all necessary measures "to preserve, maintain and re-establish a sufficient diversity and area of habitat"[2] for all birds by the creation of protected areas or biotopes and the upkeep, management and re-establishment of biotopes.

Habitats are also protected under Directive 92/43/EC (Habitats Directive). This directive "forms the cornerstone of Europe's nature conservation policy" and provides for the creation of a European network of special areas of conservation, which is also known as Natura 2000. It protects over 200 different types of habitats of particular ecological value listed in Annex 1. Moreover, it needs that habitat for those fauna and flora species which are listed in an Annex 11 be designated by Member States. In accordance with this directive, States have to establish national lists of sites, which are important for the conservation of habitat types or flora species (Sites of Community Interest). Along these national lists, the Commission also has the power to establish a list of sites of European (transnational) importance.

Although the delay they have arisen during last decades, Directive 2009/147/EU and 92/43/EC constitute the first serious attempt to conserve nature and protect sites in Western Europe.

---

1 The following environmental conventions belong to this group of conventions of nature conservation: (a) Bonn Convention of 23 June 1979 on the conservation of migratory species of wild animals; (b) Rio de Janeiro Convention of 5 June 1992 on biological diversity; (c) Salzburg Convention of 7 November 1991 on the protection of the Alps; (d) Camberra Convention of 20 May 1980 on the Conservation of the Antarctic marine living resources; (e) Paris Convention of 17 June 1994 on combating desertification.

2 Art. 3.

## 2.3 Water Pollution

Water policy has long since been one of the most important and far-reaching areas of European legislation. The "Drinking Water Abstraction Directive" (75/440/EEC) and "Bathing Water Directive" (76/166/EEC) are very early pieces of EU environmental legislation, aimed primarily at ensuring public health. These directives fixed parameters with which surface water used for the abstraction of drinking water and bathing water had to comply.
The long history of the regulation of water is characterized by fragmentation: types of water use, types of pollutant, types of potentially polluting activity have been addressed one by one, possibly by different regulators with different approaches and different enforcement powers.
Directive 80/778/EEC, adopted in 1980, five years after the proposal of the European Commission, limited the presence of undesirable substances in drinking water. This directive fixed maximum admissible concentration for 62 substances in drinking water, and gave non-mandatory guide values for some of them; Member States had to take necessary measures to ensure compliance with the concentrations.
Since there were difficulties in complying with the first directive's requirements in 1995, the European Commission decided to put forward a proposal for a new directive. The directive of 1980 was repealed and replaced by Directive 98/83/EC. The new measure provided that drinking water, at the point of entry into the domestic distribution system, must be wholesome and clean. One of the most important consequences of the change is that individuals can no longer argue against the water supply companies that their tap water must be in compliance with the European Directive. In addition, the directive requires Member States to regularly monitor the quality of water intended for human consumption and publish a report every three years on the quality of drinking water.
Directive 76/464/EEC fixed the framework conditions for discharges of dangerous substances into waters. This measure had the ambitious objective of regulating potential aquatic pollution by thousands of chemicals already produced in Europe at that time. The directive covered discharges to inland surface waters, territorial waters, inland coastal waters and ground water. In 2000, this directive was repealed by Directive 2006/11/EC on "pollution caused by certain dangerous substances discharged into the aquatic environment of the Community".
European legislation on water also covers other sectors, such as bathing water (Directives 2006/7/EC and 76/160/EEC) and groundwater quality (Directives 2006/118/EC, 2000/60/EC and 80/68/EEC).

## 2.4 Air Pollution

The third sector to mention is "air pollution". Since the early 1980s, the question of air pollution has entered the orbit of European community legislation more and more.

The concept of emissions has long since been used by Member States (mainly in legislation in Germany). According to these rules, large industrial installations in specific sectors were to operate on the basis of a permit that was to impose the best available technology without entailing excessive costs. European-wide emission limit values were elaborated first in Directives 80/779/EEC, 82/884/EEC and 85/203/EEC, respectively concerning air quality limit values and guide values for sulphur dioxide and suspended particulates, limit values for lead in the air and air quality standards for nitrogen dioxide. Despite the elaboration of these directives, the EU moved away from this concept and more or less implicitly took the decision that emission standards for industrial installations in the European Community should not be harmonized.[3] The turning point of this legislation was reached with the adoption of two directives, 96/61/EC and 96/62/EC. The first provided for the repeal of Directive 80/360/EEC. The second is also known as the Framework Directive on Air. This directive established the legal frame for setting quality standards on air pollution and which was, via other directives, progressively put into operation. Article 7 prescribes measures for Member States. They "shall draw up action plans indicating the measures to be taken in the short term where there is a risk of the limit values and/or alert thresholds being exceeded, in order to reduce that risk and to limit the duration of such an occurrence". These plans, varying according to the individual case, "provide for measures to control and, where necessary, suspend activities, including motor-vehicle traffic, which contribute to the limit values being exceeded".

Subsequent daughter Directives 1999/30/EC, 2000/69/EC and 2002/3/EC combine most of the previous provisions and add some new elements. The fourth air quality daughter Directive 2004/107/EC was to be merged later through a simplified codification process. Directive 2008/50/EC on ambient air quality and cleaner air for Europe was adopted in May 2008. It set upper and lower assessment thresholds for sulphur dioxide, nitrogen dioxide and oxides of nitrogen, particulate matter (PM10). The directive also includes the possibility for derogations from limit values in specific areas.

Policies, strategies and measures concerning air pollution are strongly influenced by a number of basic factors that need to be considered. First, air emissions stem in particular from the combustion of fuels, and the energy policy within the EU on the use of energy – nuclear energy, oil gas, coal and lignite – varies considerably, depending also on the national availability of energy sources. Second, air emissions cannot be regarded separately from other environmental problems; while, for instance, nuclear energy does not emit significant quantities of air pollutants, it has numerous other environmental and other disadvantages. Third, air emission quantities largely depend on the level of economic

3 A. Heritier, C. Knill, & S. Mingers, *Ringing the Changes in Europe: Regulatory Competition and Redefinition of the State. Britain, France, Germany*, Berlin: W. de Gruyter 1996.

development, which continues to vary considerably between Member States and makes common solutions difficult. Finally, and perhaps the most important, there seems to be no readiness in Western European society to question present lifestyles, particularly private passenger and truck transport.

## 2.5 Waste

Waste issues played a role in EU environmental policies from its very beginnings. The EU dimension of waste management problems fully came into the open with the incident of the "Seveso" barrels occurred in 1982.
The Waste Framework Directive (2008/98/EC) repealed Directive 2006/12/EC of the European Parliament and of the Council of 5 April 2006 on waste (the codified version of Directive 75/442/EEC as amended), Directive on Hazardous Waste (91/689/EEC) and the Waste Oils Directive 75/439/EEC. It provides for a general framework of waste management requirements and sets the basic waste management definitions for the EU.
Directive 2008/98/EC fixed the prevention of waste generation as the first priority for waste legislation and waste management. The aim was "breaking the link between economic growth and the environmental impacts associated with the generation of waste" (Art. 29). It obliged Member States to set up waste prevention programmes (Art. 29) and offered, in Annex IV, a list of sixteen measures that could form part of such programmes. The programmes are to be regularly updated.
In addition, it must be remembered that the EU has regulated a number of waste streams. The purpose of the provisions is to promote waste recycling and recovery, safe disposal of waste and to ensure that different national provisions on waste management do not unnecessarily affect the integrated rules on the free circulation of goods.

## 2.6 Horizontal Directives

Along with directives in specific sectors, there are also directives on subjects that cut across other environmental legislation and the environmental media such as water, air or soil. This horizontal legislation is procedural in character and provides for methods and mechanisms aimed at improving decision-making, legislative development and implementation. Horizontal EU legislation on the environment comprises five major areas of legislation. First, the Access to Information Directive (2003/4/EC) on public access to environmental information and repealing Council Directive 90/313/EEC. The Access to Information Directive was adopted by the EU in order to implement the Aarhus Convention, signed on 25 June 1998, in particular the pillar related to access to environmental information. The EU and 24 Member States are parties to this convention. The aim of the Access to Information Directive is to further the goal of contributing to a greater awareness of environmental matters by guaranteeing members of public, without their having to state an interest, the right of access to environmental information held by or for public authorities and set out the basic terms, conditions of and practical arrangements for its exercise, and ensuring that environmental information is progressively made available and disseminated to the public, in particular by computer technology.

Second, the Environmental Impact Assessment Directive (85/337/EEC) on the assessment of the effects of certain public and private projects on the environment as amended by Directive 97/11/EC.

Third, the Strategic Environmental Assessment Directive (2001/42/EC) on the assessment of the effects of certain plans and programmes on the environment.

Fourth, the Directive providing for public participation in EIA (2003/35/EC) providing for public participation with respect to the drawing up of certain plans and programmes relating to the environment and amending with regard to public participation and access to justice (85/337/EEC and 96/61/EC).

Finally, the Reporting Directive (91/692/EEC) on the implementation of certain directives relating to the environment. The aim of this directive is to rationalize and improve the way in which information is transmitted to the Commission.[4]

### 2.7 Conclusion

At the end of this analysis, we can draw some final observations on European environmental directives. The first observation is about the body of EU environment legislation. Even from my short overview it is clear how it is broad and ambitious, covering such issues as climate change, air quality, waste management, protection of water resources and biodiversity, controls on chemicals and environmental impact assessment. The second observation regards the comprehensive strategy of the EU in the fields studied. For every sector, the European Commission has begun to adopt framework directives in order to give Member States a more clear and fixed legislation. The third consideration covers the tendency of European political institutions to correct and to improve directives as the process of enforcement is taking shape. The power of implementation has not been used only to convince Member States to apply European rules but also to improve legislation in every environmental sector.

4 Most directives – with the exclusion of the Bathing Water Directive – require reports to the Commission every three years.

# 3 Mechanisms for Implementing EU Law at State Level

*Pietro Falletta and Nicola Lupo**

## 3.1 Introduction

Till the recent approval of Law 234/2012 ("General Norms on the Italian participation to the formation and implementation of European Union (EU) law and policies", published on *Gazzetta Ufficiale* of 4 January 2013), the main tool used to adapt Italian law to its EU obligations remained the annual "Community law".

Thanks to this tool, Italy, since its introduction with Law 86/1989 and up until the early 2000s, showed that it could effectively cope with the challenging obligations deriving from the process of European integration, especially in the field of arrears recovery and allowing for the acceleration that resulted from the completion of the internal market. This tool, which is by necessity inter-sectoral just like all "annual laws", has in fact allowed the impact of numerous and heterogeneous directives adopted each year to be transposed, and for an indirect objective to be politically imposed on the agenda of Parliament and the Government.

For some years now, numerous signs of inefficiency in relation to the transposition of EU law have emerged. An explanation to this can be identified, on the one hand, with the over-riding inadequacy of the "Community law"; on the other hand, with the considerable change in the overall context of law-making.

With regard to the former, there are now chronic delays in the shaping of the annual law. In fact, the presentation of the relative bill from the Government takes place with increasing delays and well after the time limit of 31 January, as it has happened in the last four years. In addition, this presentation often overlaps the process of parliamentary exam of the previous year bill, which is sometimes approved by the two Chambers later than a year since its presentation by the Government.

With regard to the second more general point, the difficulties encountered in the legislative process regarding the annual "Community law" derive from a context of overall transformation of the law-making processes, as well as from a crisis of the ordinary legislative

---

* The work is the result of close collaboration between the two authors. However, the Sections 3.1 and 3.5 were written by Nicola Lupo, while the others were written by Pietro Falletta.

procedure. The noted inefficiency of the annual "Community law" should in fact be placed, first of all, within the context of the current problems affecting the main "annual laws", such as the simplification law and the law on competition and market. The point is that, especially in the last two parliamentary terms (2006-2008; 2008-2013), for what concerns the most important legislative decisions, the ordinary legislative procedure has routinely been circumvented by the use of "omnibus" decree-laws (and their converting laws), whose parliamentary approval takes place, thanks to the intense use of maxi-amendments on which the Government requests a vote of confidence. The remedy to these signs of inefficiency has produced little effect so far: in particular, further regulatory action with respect to annual "Community law" has proliferated, *i.e.* "*ad hoc* laws" and, above all, "Community decree-laws", which have become real and proper "parallel sources" of transposition, adopted in urgency by the Government to prevent the initiation of infringement procedures.

The brief observations made so far seemed to steer towards an inevitable review of the processes of adaptation to the EU law. A strong reform of Law 11/2005 – which took place during the last parliamentary terms and ended with the approval of Law 234/2012 – appeared to be even more necessary after the entry into force of the Lisbon Treaty, on 1 December 2009. In fact, notwithstanding the individual dysfunctions mentioned above, the inadequacy of the Italian legal system in keeping pace with the EU obligations is the result of a serious delay in the compliance with the basics and innovative tools present in the new EU treaties.

In this regard, decision-making processes of the EU create a sort of competition among national legal orders by imposing new functions on Member States, as well as more penetrating forms of participation in the process of European integration. In this context, it is essential to guarantee to the Parliament a strong role throughout the entire EU decision-making process. Indeed, the ability to synthesize and systemize the different institutional, political and economic elements of the country (also in the different sections of the Government, which is not always able to identify an effective point of synthesis) lies precisely with national bicameral parliament and, therefore, in the ability to select the most sensitive and important issues to be included or considered in EU policies.

The scenario mentioned so far also seems to be the backdrop to the dynamics of environmental issues, an area where, for decades, a problematic interplay has developed between the EU regulatory path and the Italian one. Protecting the environment has in fact inspired a constant and continuous flow of directives that have had an impact on specific environmental areas, but also on a range of subjects which overlap with environmental protection requirements. The adaptation to the environmental obligations imposed by the EU certainly suffers from the aforementioned inefficiencies, which are further exacerbated by specific characteristics related to the governance of the matter in question.

First of all, the interconnection between legislations with different origins is made even more difficult by a division of legislative competences, which is still largely unclear. The result is a constant conflict between the subjects of the national system, namely State and regions, on the interpretation of the Article 117 of the Constitution, as redrafted in 2001, which has helped to undermine the aforementioned requirements of synthesis and political cohesion and therefore weakened the penetration of the Italian position within European policies.

What has been and continues to be even more serious is the uncertainty as to the correct transposition of EU law that, not coincidentally, is the predominant cause of the infringement procedures, which are still in progress.

In the following analysis, we will try to identify more specifically the weaknesses of the existing mechanisms for the adaptation to the EU legislation, and to indicate some appropriate solutions for improving Italy's ability to play a pivotal role in the EU decision-making process. As the present essay was drafted in Autumn 2012, before the approval of Law 234/2012, the analysis conducted does not consider its content. However, in order to provide a necessary update, some notes on the provisions of this new fundamental act (for the part concerning the analysis) have been formulated in the Afterword: these notes will actually confirm some of the indications derived from our analysis.

## 3.2 General Aspects of the Implementation of EU Law

The main issues in the implementation of EU law are almost all related to the "time factor". A delay which is now chronic in the presentation of "Community Bills" and in the subsequent approval of the final "Community Law" constitutes a serious characteristic of the system, which may itself bring about the initiation of infringement procedures by the Commission. According to Article 260(3) TFEU, the sanction may be applied by the Court of Justice already in the infringement procedure, if the non-fulfilment consists in the failure to notify the "measures transposing a directive adopted under a legislative procedure" by a Member State.

In fact, the risks of an excessive lengthening of the time needed for the approval of a "Community law" have been taken into account in the most recent annual laws. First of all, starting with the 2007 "Community Law", the provision for a different time limit for the implementation of draft legislation (no longer the same for all the directives set out in the annex, but directly connected to the time limit for the transposition of each directive) was introduced and then confirmed by the "Community Laws" of 2008 and 2009. In essence, for the directives which contain an indication of the time limit for transposition, the legislative decrees should be adopted within the time limits laid down in the directive. For the directives that do not include a time limit for transposition, the legislative decrees

must be enacted within twelve months from the coming into force of the "Community Law". Finally, for directives whose transposition time limit has already expired or expires within three months from the date of entry into force of the "Community Law", the legislative decrees must be enacted within three months from the entry into force of the law.
A different system, consisting in reducing the time limit for enacting the legislative decree, by identifying it two months earlier than the transposition time limit of each directive, was conceived in the "Community bills" of 2010 and 2011. Nevertheless, the abovementioned mechanism did not manage to be adopted, since the former bill was approved with many amendments (at the end of a very peculiar legislative process) and the latter stopped with the end of the legislative term.
Therefore, particularly in recent years, the legislature has been well aware of the risk of increasing delays in the transposition of EU directives that are about to reach their time-limit. But this delay is still the responsibility both of the Parliament and of the Government, as it is shown by the late submission of the "Community bill" and by the late parliamentary approval of the "Community Law", that both thwart the accelerating measures introduced by the law. When – as it was the case of the 2011 "Community bill" – there is an eight month delay in presenting the bill, the result of a prompt transposition seems already very difficult to achieve. Therefore, a reflection on the need for greater institutional correctness and a more fruitful dialogue between Parliament and the Government is inevitable, and should lead to realize a full collaboration and a concerted identification of the national priorities, starting from the drafting of EU proposals.
Currently, there is the tendency to follow a different path to solve emergencies that are due to a delayed transposition, namely the adoption of the above-mentioned "Community decree-laws". It is a remedy that goes in the opposite direction from the aforementioned one, that is of fostering dialogue and collaboration between the two Chambers and the Government. The increasing use of the emergency decree-laws enacted by the Government clearly identifies the weakness of the adaptation system, since it resorts to a legal artifice, such as the adoption of a decree, whose extraordinary necessity and urgency lies solely in the need to avoid infringement procedures from being initiated. This is due to the inability to understand a phenomenon that should be addressed with a spirit of cooperation and planning, right from the beginning of the EU decision-making processes. On the other hand, the Parliament is once again forced to ratify choices which are often hasty and incidental.
In other words, a middle ground needs to be identified between the complex and time-consuming legislative process, on one side, and the Executive impetus, which is far too decisional, on the other. Such a balance should be able to safeguard the role of both national institutions, the Parliament and the Executive, and put them in a position so as to adequately determine the identification of national priorities and to fully understand their connections with those of other countries.

This is a path which has already been laid out in the legislation of previous years and which, as we have already mentioned, has progressively corrected the system of adaptation to EU law. It has already accounted, not only for the aforementioned "time factor", but also for a more solid and comprehensive cooperation between Parliament and Government, in order to strengthen the process of participation in the shaping of European legislation, right from the outset.

### 3.3 The Forms of Coordination Between Parliament and Government

The delays and uncertainties that increasingly characterize the approval of the annual "Community Law" do not affect only the failed implementation due to the lack of transposition of the EU law, but also have important consequences on the infringement, which is to date more consistent both in the number of and reason for the infringement procedures, namely the lack or incorrect implementation of the EU law.

In this regard, the violation of the obligations imposed by the EU, even when it results directly from an administrative failure on the part of the regions or local authorities, often stems from an incorrect or inadequate framing of state legislation that should have clarified the exact scope of those obligations.

Also in this respect, it is essential that there is a significant strengthening of the forms of reconciliation between Parliament and Government, starting from the so-called "ascending phase" (that is, during the drafting of EU law). In fact, it is only through the systematic and coordinated examination of draft EU legislative proposals that a poor implementation of the obligations arising from EU law can be prevented, maybe even by managing to ensure that EU legislative acts are drafted in the light of the legal and regulatory framework in force in Italy.

The changes made in recent years to the Law 11/2005 – before its complete reform, approved in 2012 (see *infra*) – introduced progressive "adjustments" in terms of forms of coordination between the Parliament and the Executive, in particular regarding the so-called "ascending phase". From Law 13/2007 (2006 "Community Law") and, above all, with Law 96/2010 (2009 "Community Law"), a series of measures to strengthen the role of the two Chambers was included with the aim of ensuring greater coordination in the framing of EU acts and, at the same time, a more successful implementation, especially from a qualitative standpoint, of EU regulatory requirements.

The most relevant innovation has been the provision of specific disclosure requirements on the part of the Government and of accountability instruments on the follow-up procedure at the European level through the indications given by the two Chambers. The 2009 "Community Law" assigned the Inter-ministerial Committee for EU Affairs the task of coordinating the policies of the Government with the views expressed by the Parliament on the same matters, in order to reduce the risk of divergent positions and thus provide a channel for discussion and a clarification of positions. The combined provisions of Article 3 of Law 11/2005 – which provides a series of disclosure obligations on proposals for new EU measures on the part of the Government, in particular with regard to the positions that the Government intends to take in the meetings of the Council and the European Council – and Article 4-*bis*, also introduced by the 2009 "Community Law", are even more significant, aiming to give a greater degree of effectiveness to parliamentary guidelines. The Government, is indeed responsible for ensuring that the position represented by Italy at the EU level takes into account the guidelines dictated by the two Chambers, giving good reasons in case of disagreement: guidelines that become at least partially binding on a political level, since the Government, if it intended to disregard them, would be required to immediately report to Parliament, providing the appropriate justification of the new position. It is, in essence, a form of participation in European affairs which is more similar to the *mandate-based* model that aims to create the ultimate convergence between the positions of the Parliament and Government, emphasizing the powers of the former and increasing the disclosure requirements of the latter.[1]

A similar aim can be deemed at the basis of the obligations that apply to the Executive in the amended Article 15 and in the new Article 15-*ter* of Law 11/2005 – which identified a total of three separate reports to be submitted periodically to the Chambers – and, above all, Article 15-*bis*, which aims to strengthen the link between Parliament and Government during the so-called "descending phase" (that is, the implementation of EU law).

Particularly, the annual governmental report on the participation in the EU (originally scheduled in Art. 15 of Law 11/2005) has been split since 2011. By 31 January, the traditional relation of the final activities of the bodies of the Union and the Government in the preceding year should be presented. This report should include the follow-up and actions taken in respect of the opinions, observations and Chambers' acts of political direction. A second report – to be submitted by 31 December of each year – is added. Through this, the Executive shall inform the Chambers of its programme guidelines with regard to three strategic priorities about the participation in the Union: namely the development of process of integration of the EU, the adoption of specific draft legislation and communication strategies.

The Article 15-*ter* of Law 11/2005, added by the 2006 "Community Law", provides for an additional quarterly report which the Government is obliged to present to the two Chambers regarding the trend of financial flows between Italy and the EU.

1 Casalena, Fasone & Lupo 2013.

The Article 15-*bis* of Law 11/2005, however, contains provisions that have a direct impact on the need for a link during the so-called "descending phase" (that is, in the implementation of the EU Law), forcing the Government to adequately inform the two Chambers of the judicial and pre-litigation proceedings which are in progress.

Additional disclosure requirements are expected from the Minister of Economy and Finance, in consultation with the Minister for European policies, who must forward quarterly reports to the two Chambers and the Court of Auditors regarding the possible financial implications of acts and procedures described above. The 2009 "Community Law" also introduced an even more stringent interval in the case of the notification of important financial information relating to infringement procedures in progress and which must be submitted every month.

Finally, it also provides that, in cases of special importance and urgency or at the request of either Chamber, the President of the Council of Ministers or the Minister for European Policies promptly transmits documents and information to the two Chambers regarding the activities and guidelines that the Government intends to adopt and an assessment of the impact on the legal system.

In contrast to the gradual transition towards a *mandate-based scrutiny* model, a further means of reconciliation was already provided by Law 11/2005, the parliamentary scrutiny reserve, which has remained unmodified by the subsequent reforms (except for Law 234/2012: see *infra*). The intention of the legislator would be to allow the two Chambers and the Government itself to "suspend" the scrutiny of a draft EU legislative act – which must be notified to the Chambers by the Government – until the relevant parliamentary bodies give their recommendations. However, perhaps due to the fact that is still possible for the Executive to proceed with the scrutiny of the legislation just twenty days after the notification of the reserve, this measure has so far been poorly implemented.

The importance of another change introduced formally by the 2009 "Community Law" is quite different. This refers to the procedure for the verification of compliance with the principle of subsidiarity pursuant to Article 4-*quater* of Law 11/2005, already widely used in practice in recent years. Also in this case, the purpose of the legislation is to enhance the coordination between the position of the Parliament and of the Government through an exchange of information which enables the two Chambers to supervise ahead of time the compliance with the principle of subsidiarity within the framing procedure of EU acts. Moreover, this exchange of information must be considered more targeted than that provided on the basis of other provisions. The importance of this mechanism is certainly significant, especially regarding environmental issues as a matter of shared competence and one which is always at the centre of continuous legal overlapping between Member States and the EU.

### 3.4 Parliament and Government in the Institutional Practice

The framework outlined so far would seem to attest to the presence of a variety of instruments, which should ensure a virtuous consequentiality, during the so-called "ascending phase", with the activity of political direction and scrutiny of Parliament towards the Government; and in the "descending phase", with a coordinating role given to Parliament, through the "Community Law", and the main normative and administrative role in implementing EU obligations assigned to the Government. However, these channels have been until now far from successful, revealing many uncertainties and showing a negative attitude towards the objectives of connection as well as coordination both between Government and Parliament and among the different governmental departments.

With regard to the "ascending phase", the poor use of parliamentary scrutiny reserve has already been mentioned: this has only been used twice in seven years. It must be pointed out that the other instruments introduced by Law 11/2005, as amended in recent years, have not had any better results, except for the procedure on the control of compliance with the principle of subsidiarity, which stimulated a strong initiative from both Chambers: in 2010 alone, the Senate approved more than seventy recommendations and the Chamber more than twenty.

With reference to the disclosure requirements, the Annual Report on Italian participation in the EU has always been presented by the Government with such a delay that the parliamentary scrutiny on the merits was of little use.

So far, the implementation of policies aimed at strengthening the link between the positions of the Parliament and the Government has also been equally inadequate, since the Government has applied those provisions in an extremely bland and uncoordinated manner, inducing the two Chambers to continue with the examination of legislative proposals and document consultation without knowing the intentions of the Executive on the matter. In essence, the transmission from the Government to the Chambers of an Information Memorandum, specifically provided by Article 4-*quater* of Law 11/2005 and containing detailed information on the position of the Executive and the impact and technical analyses of the EU legislative proposals, is missing. This document should be flanked by a specific selection of the most relevant proposals that should be put under parliamentary scrutiny.

The critical situation which we have reported so far was subject to a separate bipartisan resolution, passed by the Chamber of Deputies on 26 July 2011 and which, among other things, committed the Government to submitting the Reports referred to in the Article 15 of Law 11/2005 within the time provided by law, and ensuring that the position represented by Italy at a EU level takes into account the guidelines defined by the two Chambers.

Parliamentary practices have so far only remedied in part to the inefficiency of the policy making instruments as required by law.

The most significant activities were carried out before the changes to the Law 11/2005, with regard to the implementation of the so-called "Barroso Strategy" – regarding compliance of the principles of subsidiarity and proportionality and the "political dialogue" – and on the experiments of the subsidiarity scrutiny measures adopted within COSAC. In this regard, the Committees on the EU Policies of the Chamber of Deputies and the Senate and the relevant committees, responsible for the subject matter, gradually increased their advisory and guiding activities as of the second half of 2008, sending to the European Commission recommendations on draft legislative acts and consultation documentation not limited only for the control on subsidiarity, but often extended to the proportionality and the merits of the acts.

However, these parliamentary procedures, which aimed at ensuring compliance with the principle of subsidiarity, in the absence of any amendments of the rules of procedure, have been fully covered by practice: in particular by a letter from the President of the Senate and by two recommendations from the Committee on the Rules in the House (the first of 6 October 2009 and the second of 14 July 2010), outlining procedures which are substantially different between the two branches of the Parliament (in particular the relations between the Committees on EU Policies and the relevant Committees), in order to approve a reasoned opinion regarding the compliance with the principle of subsidiarity.

Again with reference to the practice, the frequent use of hearings by Italian parliamentary committees of EU Commissioners and members of the European Parliament, as well as representatives of other EU institutions and bodies should be noted. There have also been parliamentary fact finding investigations on matters of European interest, debates with the competent Ministers on the activities and proposals of the EU and inter-parliamentary meetings organized by European bodies (such as the Committee on Civil Liberties, Justice and Home Affairs of the European Parliament) or National Parliaments (such as the subcommittee for examination of draft EU legislation within the Standing Committee on EU Policies of the Italian Chamber of Deputies).

A sporadic application of the aforementioned disclosures required by the new Article 15-*bis* of Law 11/2005 on infringement procedures can also be noted. There is, first of all, a strong reluctance of the Government to submit the files relating to infringement procedures to the two Chambers. In addition, the lack of cooperation between Parliament and Government is caused by the almost exclusive dialogue that the Executive has with the European Commission in the course of pre-litigation and litigation stages.

In this regard, with specific reference to a number of infringement procedures in environmental matters, it should be noted that all the formal and informal contacts between Italy and the EU institutions are maintained by the Ministry of the Environment, and in particular by the legislative office of the Ministry, through the Department for European Policies. The same goes for the EU Pilot system, a project by the European Commission operating since 2008, which introduces a negotiation in which the Commission notifies the Member States the incorrect application of EU law, prior to an infringement procedure. In this case, the Commission's dialogue primarily occurs with the Government which, however, is not even required to inform the Chambers via the channels provided by Article 15-bis of Law 11/2005, because it cannot be qualified as information relating to real infringement procedures.

Basically, once an infringement procedure has been initiated, the link between Parliament and the Government is almost non-existent. The creation of the Eur-Infra database (<http://eurinfra.Politichecomunitarie.it>), a national digital archive of infringement procedures, by the Department for European Policies at the prime minister's office at the beginning of 2008 may prove to be useless, at least from a parliamentary perspective, in the absence of an effective information of the Chambers in the pre-litigation and in the litigation stages of the procedures.

## 3.5 CONCLUSIONS

Ultimately, the set of new laws which have been mentioned so far has certainly aimed at strengthening the link between the Government and Parliament in the shaping and implementation of EU acts. However, this system has produced quite disappointing results.

The proper functioning of this inter-institutional cooperation between national Governments and national Parliaments – in particular within the EU decision-making process – can be considered, in fact, both a founding element of European democracy (as recognized by Art. 10 TEU) and an essential precondition to ensuring that Italian interests can be adequately enforced at European level. All Member States' legal systems have been called upon to adapt their structural characteristics and their decision-making processes, thus giving rise to what it is often addressed as the "Europeanization" of national institutions.[2]

The fact that, particularly after the entry into force of the Lisbon Treaty, national parliaments have direct channels of dialogue with the EU institutions does not deny the need for coordination between the Government and Parliament.[3] In fact, these direct channels have been set up and reinforced with a dual purpose: on the one hand, the prevention of national Governments from keeping the parliamentary institutions out of the loop and ending up warding off the EU's action by national public opinion; on the other, the insurance that national parliaments are able to make themselves heard on the most delicate cases and on which government action alone may be insufficient or inadequate.

In this logic, as already noticed,[4] national parliaments are no longer the victims but the protagonists of the process of European integration. And the so-called "descending phase"

2 Raunio-Wiberg 2010.
3 Casalena-Fasone-Lupo 2013.
4 O'Brennan-Raunio 2007.

would appear "less dramatic", since the main political issues and the administrative ties would already be spotted and debated in the Chambers.
In Italy, however, despite some provisions and some practices that are moving in the right direction, the picture still seems unsatisfactory:[5] the logic of urgency and forced execution continues to prevail; and the same provisions appear to be more the result of a momentarily inspired legislator rather than a coherent design.
This is demonstrated by, among other things, the many difficulties that – at the parliamentary level and even more so at the governmental level – arise in adapting the features of the annual "Community Law" to the changing characteristics of the EU and of the same national system (especially after the constitutional reform of Title V of the Constitution IN 2001). Another demonstration is given also by the many obstacles that hinder the approval of updated rules of procedure of the Chamber of deputies and Senate. In this way, the Members of Parliament seem to be considered as a hindrance rather than a useful institutional resource on which pressure can be put in order to define a national position on the policies that are being discussed at a European level.
In the end, the most effective way for correct transposition and full implementation of European legislation seems to be that of increasing the participation of the two Chambers during the so-called "ascending phase", in full accordance with guidelines and information with the Government. In this regard, it is probably no coincidence that since 2005 parliamentary scrutiny of EU draft legislation has gradually increased and, at the same time, the number of infringement procedures against Italy has gradually reduced to almost half. This simple empirical fact should, of course, lead to reflections being made on the importance of an *omnibus law*, such as the "Community Law", perhaps accompanied by other legislative acts on homogeneous sectors that at times are affected by European legislation, as much to correct transposition of directives as for preventive action against future breaches of Government. In the same vein, there is also a clear need for stronger coordination between Parliament and the Government and with regard to other institutional levels across the country, in order to define and share national priorities as soon as possible, and thus compete successfully on the European scene.

## 3.6 Afterword. The New Forms of Transposition and Implementation of EU Law, According to Law 234/2012

Some of the abovementioned complexities related to the process of transposition of the EU law have been addressed and, in part, adjusted with the approval of a new Law 234/2012, that integrally replaces Law 11/2005, in particular reforming some of the tools provided there.

5 Fabbrini-Piattoni 2008; Bindi 2011.

The approach now followed by the legislator aims to strengthen the link between the Parliament and the Government: this is as true in regard to the formation of the Italian position within EU decision-making, as it is in relation to the process of transposition and implementation of EU legislation.

The reasons for the reform – which is largely the result of legislative activity and parliamentary investigation of Committees on the EU Policies of the Chamber of Deputies and the Senate – are essentially two.

The most immediate one is the need to adapt the domestic legislation to the entry into force of the Lisbon Treaty, and, in particular, to the new centrality acquired by national Parliaments in European decision-making processes. In connection with this requirement, there is a second one, more general, of putting in place a more efficient system of participation in making and implementing European policies. For this reason, the system should be based on the strengthening of the political direction and scrutiny powers of the Parliament, in parallel to the experiences of other Member States.

Ultimately, the new balance created by the Lisbon Treaty among the EU institutions and between them and the Member States, made necessary a greater democratic legitimacy of the decisions taken at the European level. This balance further imposed therefore a redefinition of the fitting tools between Parliament and Government in the direction of a higher incidence of parliamentary scrutiny over the activities of the executive.

With regard to the "ascending phase", the main objective of the law is to strengthen the Parliament's role in the process of formation of the Italian position. This will be based on the experience that the positions with a strong support of the Parliament are most often those with the highest probability of penetration and success in the EU decision-making.

The major novelties are as follows: the informative duties of the Government before the Chambers are strengthened; a better specification of the conditions for the activation of parliamentary scrutiny reservation; the prerogatives granted to the Chambers by the Lisbon Treaty, which are also regulated for their internal profiles.

For what concerns the informative duties, the pre-existing rules are renewed by requiring the Government to promptly inform the competent parliamentary bodies about the initiatives related to the Common Security and Defense Policy (CSDP) submitted to the Council (or currently at issue), giving special emphasis to those which have implications on the defence. There is a similar obligation to prompt information in case of the conclusion of agreements among EU Member States providing the introduction or the strengthening of the rules on financial or monetary matters. Similar duties follow the conclusion of agreements which determine major impact on public finances, even outside the provisions of the treaties.

More generally, the new provisions are intended to enhance the overall disclosure obligations of the Government in relation to the work of the EU institutions, even compared to the prevailing informal activities, thanks to the support of notes and reports of the Permanent Representation to the EU that make the Parliament aware of the actual progress of the negotiations at the European level. In this regard, the role of the Permanent Representation is fundamental for the realization of the aforementioned objective of strengthening parliamentary intervention in European politics, since communications on informal activities and investigations by the EU institutions are essential to understanding the scope for intervention and definition of Italian position and the actual consistency of the Government with respect to parliamentary guidelines.

However, the most important novelty is contained in the Article 6 of Law 234/2012, according to which the Government is expected to accompany the EU draft legislation, "in cases of particular relevance", with an explanatory note of assessment. These notes, submitted within twenty days from the reception of the document, shall provide for a technical report on the compliance with the EU competences, together with prospects for negotiation and impact assessment on the internal organization. Of great importance is the prediction that the technical report is accompanied by a table of correspondence between the provisions of the draft and the applicable national rules. The analysis of this table would allow a more careful analysis of the impact of European legislation on our system, with obvious benefits both in the phases of negotiations and implementation and transposition of EU obligations. The previous rule foresaw only a report on the compliance with the subsidiarity principle upon a parliamentary request, whereas the new Law ensures a broader and better specified information of the Parliament, which will constantly receive information.

With regard to the parliamentary scrutiny reservation on pieces of the EU draft legislation at issue, it will not be posed systematically, but upon the request of any of the Chambers. The Government can always request the reserve under its own initiative on acts of particular political, economic and social importance. However, the Government may keep on debating the measures at the EU level even in absence of a parliamentary decision. The term for the parliamentary reserve has been increased to thirty days. In the end, the new discipline acknowledges the insufficiency of the institute as a measure of the steady parliamentary scrutiny on governmental activities. Consequently, minor improvements are being introduced for a more balanced application in specific cases.

With reference to the prerogatives of the Chambers related to the simplified procedures of revision of the treaties (as well as to those EU decisions whose enter into force requires the approval by the Member States), the role of the Chambers has been clearly strengthened, following the provisions of the Lisbon Treaty. In particular, the active participation of the Chambers is ensured by requiring the joint decision by the two Chambers on these proceedings (in some cases through a legislative act), trying to be coherent with the functioning of the Italian symmetrical bicameralism. For instance, the decisions of the European Council on the simplified revision of the treaties and common defence policy have to be approved by means of a parliamentary statute (passed by both Chambers), following the proposal introduced by the Government within thirty days from the European Council decision.

Moreover, Article 12 of Law 234/2012 introduces the mechanism of the "emergency brake", according to which the Italian representative in the Council must ask for the submission to the European Council of draft legislative acts concerning social security, mutual recognition of judgments and definition of criminal offences and sanctions in the areas of particularly serious crime, upon a reasoned motion passed by both Chambers. Moreover, in cases in which the Treaty on EU provides that the Council shall act by a qualified majority voting-system (Art. 31, para. 2, TUE), the Chambers may adopt a reasoned motion in order to ask the Italian representative in the Council to oppose the decision, for vital and stated reasons of national policy. Finally, the "emergency brake" might be decided also autonomously by the Government, in case the Chambers do not express any position within the given term of thirty days.

Further innovations are related to the subsidiarity check, giving implementation to the provisions of the Lisbon Treaty, and in particular of the Article 6 of the Protocol No. 2 on the application of the principles of subsidiarity and proportionality. The procedure for the expression of the reasoned opinion (to be sent to the EU Parliament, Council and Commission) will be provided by the parliamentary rules of procedure. It is also foreseen that the reasoned opinion has to be sent at the same time also to the Government, in order to involve the latter in the scrutiny procedure and, at the same time, to avoid diverging views between Italian institutions within the EU. However, these procedures will remain not fully effective until the approval of a comprehensive reform of the parliamentary rules of procedure on this matter, in order to formalize, standardize and better articulate the current procedures based on the mentioned practices.

Dealing with the "descending phase", the new law inevitably attempts to respond to the unrelenting decline of the efficacy of the annual Community Law, outlined in the previous paragraphs, and now confirmed also by the failure to approve the 2011 Community Law before the end of the XVI parliamentary term. In addition, it is worth to mention the controversial story of the so-called "save infringements" decree-law (DL 216/2012: "Urgent provisions aimed at avoiding the application of sanctions from the European Union"), that shows how the Government is not able to respond to the infringement procedures without the parliamentary support. This decree-law was initially adopted in a first version (containing the measures to close 21 different infringement procedures, some of them likely to bring to sanctions); then, it was approved in a new reduced version (that included only four proceedings, leaving out many important subjects related to environmental law, such as environmental damage and hunting activity); finally, the bill of indemnity presented for the conversion of the decree-law risked not be approved because of the end of the parliamentary term and it had to be transformed into an amendment to the stability bill (Law 228/2012: Art. 1, paras 324-362).

In the light of these serious difficulties in the reception of the EU law, the innovations introduced by Law 234/2012 aim therefore to realize a solid and structural intervention in a field that strongly needed it. In brief, the reception procedure has been reshaped in a double track that includes two different tools: the "European delegation Law" and the "European law".

The European delegation Law has been thought as an evolution of the former model of the annual Community law. It will consist in a parliamentary act of delegation to the Government in order to implement the directives whose term of transposition is close (or even gone). The responsibility of the proceedings lies with the President of the Council of Ministers or the Minister for European Policies, who must submit to the Chambers the bill of delegation by 28 February of each year. In continuity with some failed attempts already tried with the annual 2010 and 2011 Community Law (see *supra*, section 3.2), there is a significant innovation regarding the terms for the transposition of the directives: the deadline for the enactment of the delegated legislation implementing directives will be scheduled two months in advance with respect to the deadline for the transposition of the same directive. In the case of further need for fulfillment of the implementing obligations, the government may submit to the Chambers, by 31 July of each year, a further bill for a new European delegation Law. This provision reveals the main concern of the Parliament, which is to intervene on inefficient regulations that may cause the opening (or the aggravation) of an infringement procedure.

This same concern is also at the basis of the second tool identified by Law 234/2012: the so-called "European law". It consists in a possible statute, without a predetermined timetable for submission and approval, to be used in cases of specific needs, and, in particular: a) to approve or amend provisions or repeal internal rules that are in conflict with the European legislation, especially if relevant in infringement procedures or related to rulings by the Court of Justice; b) to give effect to acts of the EU and the international treaties concluded by the EU; c) to replace provisionally regional and local measures in case of delay or failure to fulfill an European obligation.

As mentioned, the new system of implementation of European legislation is characterized by the clear intention to prevent or react to the EU infringement procedures. This is also testified by the provision on parliamentary oversight on infringement procedures concerning Italy (Art. 15 of Law 234/2012), which asks the Government to transmit to both the Chambers a report explaining the reasons that led to the (alleged) breach thereof and the actions to be taken for a positive solution of the procedure. The Government is asked also for: i) providing for the reasons that caused the failure in implementing one or more European acts; and ii) reporting periodically on the status of implementation of directives (Art. 39 of Law 234/2012).

In sum, an appreciable effort in order to strengthen the legislature and to face the chronic delays in implementing EU law has been surely undertaken. The so-called "European law"

may in particular help to restore the proper centrality of Parliament and, therefore, to achieve a more balanced relationship with the Government. In addition, it may facilitate the construction of a more efficient procedural framework in responding to emergency in the implementation phase, replacing the more complex and time-consuming procedure of delegated legislation and the other disadvantages of the decree-laws.
However, a risk of inefficiency remains in the background: there is the potential overlap between the "European law", the "European delegation law" and further possible measures, considering also the recognized possibility for the Government to introduce individual bills for the implementation of specific EU acts (see Art. 38 of Law 234/2012), as well as to adopt decree-laws on this subject. Finally, an ultimate risk concerns the lack of an actual institutional dialogue between the Parliament and the Government, beyond the procedures framed in the new law: even these new tools may remain non-enforced or self-referential without an effective cooperation between the two institutions at the political as well as at the administrative level.

## REFERENCES

F. Bindi, *Italy and the European Union*, Washington D.C.-Rome, 2011.

J. O'Brennan & T. Raunio (Eds.), *National Parliaments within the Enlarged European Union. From 'Victims' of Integration to Competitive Actors?*, London-New York, 2007.

P. Casalena, C. Fasone & N. Lupo, 'Commentary on the Protocol No. 1 annexed to the Treaty of Lisbon ("On the role of national Parliaments in the European Union")', *in* Blanke & Mangiameli (Eds.), *Commentary on the Treaty of European Union*, Berlin-New York, 2013, forthcoming.

S. Fabbrini & S. Piattoni, *Italy in the European Union: Redefining National Interest in a Compound Polity*, Lanham, 2008.

T. Raunio & M. Wiberg, 'How to Measure the Europeanisation of a National Legislature?', 33 *Scandinavian Political Studies*, 1, 2010, pp. 74-92.

# 4 The Implementation of EU Law at Regional Level

*Giovanni Di Cosimo*

## 4.1 The Regions

The Italian Constitution of 1948 introduced regions as an intermediate level of government between central government and local government formed by municipalities and provinces. The Italian regions were endowed with statutory, legislative, administrative and financial autonomy. The first two forms of autonomy are the most characterizing: on the one hand through the adoption of regions' charters (*statuti regionali*), each region determines its own form of government and the basic principles of organization and work;[1] on the other hand, through legislation. Regions express their own policies which must, however, comply with those at national level (a reason for which regional lawmakers can never exceed the limits and boundaries of legislative principles set by the state). The Constitution also confers the *task of contributing to the implementation of EU legislation to the regions* although this competence lies primarily with the State. The intervention of the regions in the implementation of EU law, which can be more or less ample depending on the cases, allows them to adapt national provisions to the different territorial realities. To this end, the regions employ various tools: regional charters, laws and administrative acts. In this chapter, we shall focus in particular on those rules adopted by the regions, in order to implement EU law, and on the mechanisms they have developed.

## 4.2 Regions' Charters and Laws

The Italian Constitution states that the regions "provide for the implementation of international agreements and European acts" (Art. 117.5). Following constitutional provisions, regions' charters include some rules for implementing EU law. For instance, the possibility for the President of the Region to ask for a vote of confidence "on the implementation acts of EU law" (Art. 49 Campania Region Charter's); or to underline the need to provide for rapid implementation;[2] or even the mandatory establishment of a Council committee for EU Community Affairs (*Commissione consiliare per gli affari comunitari*).[3] Abrogative referendums

1 The regions are provided with a legislative body, the Regional Council and with an Executive body, the Regional Parliament, chaired by the President of the region who is elected directly.
2 Art. 10.4 Region's Charter Lazio.
3 Art. 32.1 Region's Charter Lazio.

are not allowed within the implementation as process in order to prevent the possibility that the referendum could result as being responsible for EU laws non-implementation.[4] At the same time, regional laws enforce regions' charters developing specific rules for the implementation of EU law (*procedural laws*).[5] The Italian Constitutional Court confirmed regional procedures of implementation in the scope of procedural laws established by national laws, saying that regions can regulate through law, "a specific internal procedure aimed at establishing the method" of implementation at a regional level (Case No. 372/2004). The relevance of procedural law is highlighted by, on one hand, the fact that regional laws can be abrogated only in a stipulated manner.[6]

## 4.3 Subjects and Pre Conditions

The regional implementation of EU law involves both the Regional Council (*Consiglio regionale*), which is the legislative body, as well as the Regional Executive (*Giunta regionale*) which is the executive body chaired by the President of the Region, who is elected directly by the inhabitants of the region. However, the executive body is better equipped to deal with this task since it has more offices and more data available. For this reason "the Council's right to precautionary and subsequent information on community affairs" is enforced and establishes that the Council committees can ask the Regional Executive to refer on the state of implementation (Arts. 42.2 and 31.3 Calabria Region's Charter). Subject to the regional government bodies acting as the main players in the implementation procedures, the independent territorial authorities (municipalities and provinces) are also involved as are economic and social authorities.[7] The Council of local government (*Consiglio delle autonomie locali*), that is a consultation body between the region and local government (municipalities and provinces) as provided by the Constitution, is also involved but only regarding some particular matters (local territorial organization, competences and attributions of local authorities, revenues and local authority expenditure).[8]
The pre condition of the implementation is the assessment of the compliance of the regional law with the EU law. Different options are available. On one hand, some regions

4 *E.g.* Art. 10.2 Liguria Region's Charter.
5 Most of the regions have their own procedural law: R.L. 44/1995 Liguria; R.L. 10/2004 Friuli Venezia Giulia; R.L. 8/2006 Valle d'Aosta; R.L. 14/2006 Marche; R.L. 3/2007 Calabria; R.L. 18/2008 Campania; R.L. 16/2008 Emilia-Romagna; R.L. 32/2008 Molise; R.L. 22/2009 Abruzzo; R.L 31/2009 Basilicata; R.L. 26/2009 Tuscany; R.L. 13/2010 Sardegna; R.L. 10/2010 Sicily; R.L. 17/2011 Lombardy; R.L. 24/2011 Puglia; R.L. 26/2011 Veneto. From this point, when a regional law is referred to without indicating the number and year, it will be a procedural law. Moreover, only a single regional act will be referred to in the examples even if this provision can be found in other regional law systems.
6 Art. 10 R.L. Friuli Venezia Giulia.
7 Art. 39.6 Lombardy Region's Charter.
8 Art. 4.3 Abruzzo Region's Charter.

establish that the assessment of non-compliance lies with the Regional Council; more precisely, they attribute the "constant assessment" of compliance to the competent Council committee.[9] On the other hand, several regions attribute the assessment to the executive body in its various components: to the Regional Executive,[10] or the President of the region,[11] or even to the regional departments which "communicate the outcomes to the President of the Region" (Art. 6.3 R.L. Region of Sicily). An alternative way of determining the state of compliance takes into consideration the administrative practices: the Regional Executive presents a bill to substitute the regional dispositions which the administration decides not to apply due to incompatibility with EU law.[12]

## 4.4 LEGISLATIVE IMPLEMENTATION

The regions have two tools to implement EU law. The first is the law that adapts the regional law following a change in EU law. Seeing as this is approved when needed, it can be defined as an *occasional law*. According to the legislative procedure the Regional Executive has to present the bill "at least three months prior to the adjustment time limit as set out in the Directive" (Art. 4.2 R.L. Liguria Region). Furthermore, in order to speed up the process, it is possible to opt for the urgent procedure which involves the reduction of preliminary reviewing and the possibility to transcribe the text in the Assembly agenda even if the Council committee has not yet completed the review within the prescribed time limits.[13]

The second tool is the law that adapts the periodic regional legal system: *Periodic law* or *Community law*.[14] Its distinctive characteristics are defined by the Region's Charter or procedural law; the yearly periodicity and the discussion in a special session of the Regional Council. Some regions add specific functional rules to this model in order to shorten the legislative procedure (we will come back to this later). However, the procedural law of the Region of Tuscany is slightly different from this model since, despite its periodicity, it does not precisely establish that the Law must be yearly and does not institute a specific session. Another distinctive characteristic of the Periodic law should be its heterogeneous content in so far as it enforces EU law of the preceding year. However, if we look at the standard

9 Art. 4 R.L. Camapania.
10 Art. 5.1 R.L. Calabria.
11 Art. 6 R.L. Veneto.
12 Art. 8.1 bis R.L. Friuli Venezia Giulia.
13 Art. 82 Int. Reg. Council of Lombardy; for the same purpose Art. 8.2 R.L. Puglia foresees the use of the priority proposal.
14 This legal tool is mentioned in Art. 8.5 of the State Law 11/2005 which refers to "yearly transposition laws". Here the two names *Periodic law* and *Community law* shall be used indifferently.

procedure, we discover that sometimes even occasional laws regulate a great variety of subjects.[15]
Observing the standard procedure, there are cases in which the Region's Charter introduces the Periodic law, although the law has not so far been effectively approved (Piemonte Region) and cases in which the regions have used this tool even if it was not provided for by the Charter (Calabria, Marche, Puglia, Tuscany, Friuli Venezia Giulia, Valle d'Aosta). Other data emerge from the standard procedure: the regions which choose the yearly periodicity may encounter difficulties in respecting it, therefore, some of them have still not adopted the Community laws.[16]
Finally, it is worth to notice that the regions which have adopted the Periodic law do not consider it as an exclusive tool.[17] Occasional laws are usually enacted when it is necessary to implement an EU act in a time of the year which does not coincide with a Community session. However, occasional laws could also be used (as an alternative to the Periodic laws) when a reform of an entire sectorial law is preferred to *ad hoc* implementation.

### 4.5 COMMUNITY LAW

Community law is discussed in a specific council work session held every year within the date previously set by the Region's Charter or procedural law (so-called "Community session"). The bill is presented annually by the President of the region, or by the Regional Executive.[18] The proposal bears the title "Regional Community law" and shows the year of reference.[19] In the report attached to the bill, the Regional Executive reports on the compliance of the Community law and on the infringement proceedings which are ascribed to the regions.[20] It also reports on the state of implementation of Community law of the previous year[21] and it lists the directives to be implemented as prescribed by regulatory or administrative rules.[22]
As mentioned before, some regions have introduced *functional rules to speed up the approval procedure* of Community law. These rules aim to predetermine the duration of the various proceeding stages, beginning with the discussion by the relevant committee with regard to relations with the EU and which must be concluded within 40 days of the bill approval.[23] Where Assembly's examination is required there are a number of possibilities

15 For example, R.L. Liguria 14/2011 which implements the Directive concerning services on the domestic market but which also contains a reference dedicated to the provisions relative to environmental matters.
16 Molise, Calabria, Sardegna, Sicily.
17 Arts. 39.1 and 5 Lombardy Region's Charter.
18 The first hypothesis is provided for by Art. 39.3 Lombardy Region's Charter; the second by Art. 3.2 R.L. Basilicata.
19 Art. 3.1 R.L. Marche.
20 Art. 3.3 R.L. Marche.
21 Art. 8.3 R.L. Veneto.
22 Art. 3.3 letter b R.L. Friuli Venezia Giulia.
23 Art. 38 Int. Reg. Emilia-Romagna.

regarding who is competent to decide. This could be the Bureau of the Regional Legislative Assembly (*Ufficio di Presidenza dell'Assemblea*), which approves the work agenda of the assembly establishing a time limit for the final voting on the proposed bill[24] or the Council President, who "sets beforehand the day and the hour of the final vote" (Art. 43.3 Piemonte Region's Charter); or even the Conference of groups of the Regional Council (*Conferenza dei gruppi consiliari*), which sets the time limit for the final vote "after which the work of the Assembly, following a majority resolution, continues beyond the scheduled timetable until all votes have been cast" (Art. 128 Int. Reg. Friuli Venezia Giulia Region). There is also the possibility of a fixed time limit, directly indicated by the procedural law.[25] It must also be pointed out that in practice the regions do not seem to follow effectively the fast track procedures, which in fact depend on the capacity of the Council majority to respect the established procedure times.[26]

As far as content is concerned, Community law sets out "provisions a) repealing or modifying regional laws in contrast with Community regulations or acts, b) implementing and enforcing the Directives and the Community acts, c) enforcing the sentences of the Court of Justice and other Council measures or those of the European Commission compelling regions to comply" (Art. 7.2 R.L. Tuscany). Other procedural laws provide further indications, in particular the indication of acts which can be implemented from an administrative standpoint and the authorization for implementation by means of regulations. However, the implementation cannot defer to such acts, and therefore the law must provide directly when "the fulfilment of Community obligations means an increase in costs and a reduction in revenues, the individuation of administrative penalties or the institution of new governing bodies" (Art. 8.3 letter h R.L. Lombardy). An annex to the law set out the directives where the Regional law is already compliant with EU law.[27]

## 4.6 Regulatory Implementation

Regions have two options to carry out regulatory implementation: 1) regulations set out by the Regional Council, and 2) those set out by the Regional Executive.

The *model of regulatory implementation by the Regional Council* allows it to make use of both of the law and the regulations, whereby the Council's preference will inevitably be

24 Art. 19.3 Int. Reg. Umbria.

25 Art. 5.1 R.L. Abruzzo according to which the law is to be approved "prior to the 31 July each year".

26 The rule of the Piemonte Region's Charter, according to which the Council President establishes the moment of the final vote, has remained on paper, because not even the legislative proceedings have been commenced; the procedural law in Abruzzo has not been respected, considering that the EU laws have been implemented after the time limit.

27 Art. 8.3 R.L. Sicilia.

that of the law. In fact in the three-year period between 2009 and 2011, only one regulation was approved in the Abruzzo Region, which, furthermore, was not related to the implementation of European directives; a somewhat modest performance compared to the 87 regulations approved over the same period by the Regional Executive of Puglia (some of which implement European laws on the environment: *e.g.* R.L. 10/2010 on the energy certification of buildings, R.L. 24/2010 on plants fuelled by renewable sources). In the Marche Region, the situation is slightly different, also because the Region's Charter, while assigning regulatory competence to the Council, unlike the Abruzzo Region's Charter allows the individual law to authorize the Regional Executive to adopt regulations, consequently, in the three-year period 16 regulations were approved, 9 of which by the Regional Executive. The *model of implementation through regulations of the Executive Committee* is suitable for the executive function that characterizes this body. In this specific framework, it is worth distinguishing between the idea that the Regional Executive can adopt the regulation only subsequent to legislative authorization (Art. 11.4 Lazio Region's Charter), from the idea that it can proceed independently from such authorization (Art. 42 Tuscany's Region Charter).

In the second hypothesis, the law can give the Council competence to implement regulations (Art. 42.1 letter c Lombardy Region's Charter), and provides for the reasoned opinion of the competent Council committee.[28] This is a way to limit Regional Executive's power to be implemented through regulations. However, in one case there is the possibility to implement the urgent procedure allowing for the acquisition of the Council committee's opinion after the adoption of the regulations (Art. 8.2 letter b R.L. Puglia).

More extensively, beyond the two hypotheses of the *general authorization* (by the Region's Charter) or by the *specific authorization* (by individual laws), the implementation of regulations by the Regional Executive is limited on the basis of various measures. First, the previously mentioned exclusion of the regulation through the discipline of certain objectives reserved to Community law. Second, the Assembly's reasoned opinion on the compliance of the regulation with respect to the Region's Charter (Art. 28.4 letter n Emilia-Romagna Region's Charter). Third, the establishment of limits by the Regional Law (Art. 49.2 Emilia-Romagna Region's Charter). Finally, the submission of the regulation for the approval of the Council (Art. 56.2 Campania Region's Charter).[29]

With regard to types of regulation, in most cases they regard implementation regulations, *i.e.* acts required to make EU law operative in regional fields. However, it is also necessary to make a distinction as to whether the regulations can directly implement the EU acts (Art. 27.4 Piemonte Region's Charter), or whether legislative intermediation is necessary, for which the regulations implement the Regional Community law which sets out criteria and principles (Art. 8.3 letter b R.L. Lombardy). In some regions, Community

28 See Reg. 5/2011 Liguria on protection of the marine environment.

29 See Reg. 1/2009 Campania on the strategic environmental assessment.

law authorizes the adoption of regulations (*regolamenti di delegificazione*) in the subject matter not covered by legal reserve (Art. 5.3 Puglia). This means that Community law determines the abrogation of the law which disciplines the subject matter of the deregulation from the moment the regulation is adopted. However, Community law establishes that the criteria the regulation must follow and significantly reduces the Regional Executive's range of action: furthermore, the Council Committee competent for the matter expresses a prior "binding opinion" on the text (Art. 5.3 R.L. Friuli Venezia Giulia).

## 4.7 Administrative Implementation

The last type of implementation consists of administrative acts. This course of action can also be divided into Acts by the Regional Executive and Acts by the Regional Council, which can be adopted according to the respective competences defined by the Region's Charter always when the implementation does not require "a prior regulation of the subject matter" (Emilia-Romagna Region's Charter, Art. 12.1 letter b).
As far as the acts of the Regional Council are concerned, it is sufficient to note that the majority is put forward by the Regional Parliament which has specialized offices available, and that they refer to "general provisions".[30]
Regarding the Regional Executive instead, there are two different options available. In the first, the Regional Executive independently chooses the acts to be implemented on the basis of a *general authorization.* One example is provided by the procedural law of the region of Tuscany according to which the Regional Executive implements the EU directives which modify "exclusively technical characteristics of Directives and of other Community acts already transposed into national or regional Community regulations" and provides "the administrative implementation of Community Acts (Art. 8 R.L. Tuscany)". Another form of general authorization is linked to the adoption of temporary acts for emergency situations: the President of the region has the power to adopt "urgent and temporary administrative precautionary measures and primary adaptation to the Community acts to be immediately enforced" (Art. 41.7 Lazio Region's Charter). A general form of authorization is also to be found in the laws on regional organization which assign the competence to issue general directives and guidelines to the bodies of political-administrative management.
In the second alternative, it is the individual law that indicates which EU laws the Regional Executive must implement administratively. The *specific authorization* is contemplated by some procedural laws which refer to the Community law for the reference to which EU acts are to be implemented administratively, setting out the relative principles and criteria,

30 Art. 33.3 letter e Veneto Region's Charter.

as well as the various time limits.[31] Naturally, the indication of the EU acts can also be implemented by occasional laws which in a few cases concede a wide time margin within which the Regional Executive can intervene.[32]

### 4.8 Sequence

The implementation process requires regions to follow specific procedures made by regulatory and administrative acts. EU laws are usually first implemented at a national level through Community laws, legislative decrees, governmental regulations, decrees by the Prime Minister, ministerial decrees etc.; subsequently they are implemented at a regional level by regional law and then by regulatory and administrative acts.
However, the combination among the acts can vary from case to case. The following two cases can serve as an example.
Case I (relating to the control of urban waste water treatment plants). There are six steps in the legal sequence: EU directives, national transposition act (environmental code), regional laws, regional regulation, resolution by the Regional Executive of Region of Lombardy, protocols between the actors involved in the control.
Case II (relating to the overseas destination of waste originating from disposal plants). A deliberation by the Regional Executive (*delibera della Giunta regionale*) of Veneto temporarily suspends the efficacy of a previous deliberation referred to an EU directive which was in the process of being transposed. Such circumstance creates a situation of interpretative uncertainty. The suspended deliberation refers to European normative acts (including those which have not yet been transposed on a national level) as well as national ones, therefore the legal sequence only goes through three stages: EU directive, national transposition act (environmental code), Regional Executive Deliberation.

31 In the first sense, see Art. 11.1 letter d R.L. Sardegna; in the second, see Art. 8.4 R.L. Lombardy.
32 *E.g.* R.L. 3/2011 Lombardy according to which the Executive Committee "sets out provisions" limiting the use of heating systems.

# 5 Infringement Proceedings

*Michela Angeli and Paolo Palchetti**

## 5.1 Introduction

Pursuant to Articles 258 and 260 TFEU, the infringement proceeding is articulated in two phases: a pre-litigation phase of administrative character; and a subsequent judicial phase. A third phase relates to the execution of the European Court of Justice (ECJ) ruling, which can impose financial penalties on the convened Member State. This chapter will provide an introduction to the principal notions related to these different phases with particular reference to the recent developments in the environment sector.

The number of ongoing procedures concerning the environment accounted for around 20% of the total, both in 2010[1] and in 2011.[2] However, the percentage dramatically increases when considering actions brought by the Commission for the imposition of financial sanctions alone. More than half of the total actions under Article 260(2) TFEU, in fact, are due to infringements of the European Union (EU) *acquis* in the environment sector.[3] In conclusion, it will be argued that, in view of the novelties introduced by the Lisbon Treaty, stronger action by the Commission against violations in this sector can be expected in the future.

## 5.2 The Pre-Litigation Phase

### 5.2.1 The Role of the Commission and of the Member States

The Commission, as "guardian of the treaties", plays a central role during the entire procedure and, in particular, during the pre-litigation phase foreseen in Article 258 TFEU.[4]

---

* Although this chapter is the result of a shared work effort by the two authors, Dr. Michela Angeli is responsible for the writing of Sections 5.1 to 5.2.4 and Section 5.4.2, Prof. Paolo Palchetti edited the remaining Sections. The authors would like to thank Mr. Ken Mifsud-Bonnici, Member of the Legal Service of the European Commission, for his valuable comments on the first draft of this chapter.

1 In particular, in 2010 one quarter of the cases due to failure to transpose directives (which in 2010 accounted for around 20% of all ongoing cases), related to the environment sector. 28th Annual Report of the Commission on the control of the application of EU Law (2010), 29.09.2011, COM(2011) 588 final, pp. 3, 4 and 7.

2 29th Annual Report of the Commission on monitoring the application of EU Law (2011), 30.11.2012, COM(2012) 714 final, p. 10.

3 *Ibid.*, pp. 10 and 11.

4 Indeed, the Commission also plays a role within the procedure foreseen in Art. 259 TFEU, which provides for the activation of the infringement proceeding by a Member State.

As provided in Article 17(1) TEU, it shall "ensure the application of the Treaties, and of measures adopted by the institutions pursuant to them". In each phase of the proceedings, the Commission has a large margin of discretion and may proceed on its own initiative or on the basis of a complaint.[5] However, it has no obligation to act, even in the presence of such a request.[6]

For their part, the Member States are held, by virtue of the principle of loyal cooperation, codified in Article 4(3) TEU, to adopt "any appropriate measure, general or particular, to ensure fulfilment of the obligations arising out of the Treaties or resulting from the acts of the institutions of the Union". On the basis of this principle, the Member States are obliged to cooperate loyally with the Commission throughout the entire procedure, in order to facilitate the achievement of the Commission's task of ensuring that Union law is applied correctly.[7]

### 5.2.2 *Object of the Proceedings*

According to Article 258 TFEU, the Commission can commence an infringement proceeding where a Member State "has failed to fulfil an obligation under the Treaties".[8] Further to primary law, this notion includes any obligations deriving from Union law.[9]

It is settled case law that the infringement procedure has an "objective nature" as it only aims to assess the consistency of Member States' conduct with regard to Union law. Hence, an alleged infringement can be contested even if it concerns only a part of the State's territory. In this respect, in the case concerning waste disposal in Campania, the Court recently ruled that

> the fact that, by the present action, the Commission is seeking a declaration that the Italian Republic has failed to fulfil its obligation to take the necessary measures only with regard to the region of Campania can have no bearing on any finding of such an infringement.[10]

5 The Commission is alone responsible to decide if and when to start or proceed to the next procedural step in the procedure, *i.e.* if to move to the next step, close the procedure or refer the matter to the ECJ.

6 In practice, it is increasingly the case that the Commission acts following the receipt of complaints from natural or legal persons who believe they have suffered prejudice as a result of national measures incompatible with Union Law. See the Communication from the Commission to the Council and the European Parliament, Updating the handling of relations with the complainant in respect of the application of Union law, COM(2012) 154 final.

7 Case C-33/90, *Commission v. Italy* [1991] ECR I-5987, para.18, where the Court stated that: "for the achievement of such a task, it is vital that the Commission should be fully informed of the measures adopted by Member States for the implementation of the provisions in question".

8 Among the derogations to this provision, Art. 275 TFEU relative to Foreign Policy and Common Security and the other acts adopted on the basis of the said provisions is of note.

9 The notion can comprise obligations deriving from International agreements concluded by the Union that are binding upon the institutions and the Member States, by virtue of Art. 216(2) TFEU. A Member State's failure to comply with a Court judgement following a preliminary ruling request pursuant to Art. 267 TFEU can also lead to an infringement proceeding.

10 Case C-297/08, *Commission v. Italy* [2010] ECR I-1749, para. 98.

In a similar line, in a case against Denmark relating to the quality of bathing water, the Court stated that "where a Member State fails to fulfil its obligations under the Treaty or under secondary legislation, the infringement exists regardless of the frequency or the scale of the circumstances complained of".[11]

A Member State's failure to cooperate in *bona fide* with the Union institution, pursuant to Article 4(3) TEU, through, for instance, a prolonged failure to respond to a Commission request for information, can represent an autonomous basis of infringement and, as such, can autonomously form the object of infringement proceedings. Furthermore, the ECJ has clarified that pursuant to this duty, whenever a State refuses to supply the Commission with the information requested, it should still be held under an obligation to explain its failure to provide that information.[12]

Lack of or incomplete transposition of directives still represent a significant number of Article 258 TFEU cases. Such infringements (often referred to as "non-communication" or "non-com" infringements) are systematically pursued by the adoption of letters of formal notice against Member States which have failed to communicate national measures adopted to implement a directive within two months from the deadlines provided for transposition.[13] Following the amendment introduced by the Lisbon Treaty to Article 260(3) TFEU, where Member States fail to notify implementing measures to the Commission, the Commission can directly request the Court to apply a penalty payment on the Member State concerned already in the first Court ruling, pursuant to Article 258 TFEU, without adopting a reasoned opinion (see *infra*).[14]

With regard to the subject of the infringement, it should be noted that the ECJ has interpreted the notion of "State" contained in Article 258 TFEU inclusively of any internal articulation this would involve. The behaviour which is the object of the procedure could therefore be subsequent to actions or omissions by central or local authorities, as well as by governmental, parliamentary or judicial bodies. According to settled case law, in fact, while each Member State may be free to allocate areas of internal legal competence as it sees fit, the fact still remains that it alone is responsible towards the Union for compliance with obligations arising under Union law.[15]

---

11 Case C-226/01, *Commission v. Denmark* [2003] ECR I-1219, para. 32.

12 Case C-33/90, *Commission v. Italy* [1991] ECR I-5987, para. 20.

13 Indeed, in "non-com" cases, the letter of formal notice is effectively proposed to the Commission automatically following identification of the late notification of a transposing measure by a computer system. The notification must concern national provisions already in force or of imminent entry into force (in the case of Italy, already published in the *Gazzetta Ufficiale*).

14 The Commission referred the first "non-com" infringement to the Court with a request for financial sanctions under Art. 260(3) TFEU in late 2011. Five Member States were involved in nine such decisions in 2011: Austria (one case), Germany (three cases), Greece (one case) Italy (one case) and Poland (three cases). The proposed daily penalty ranged from € 44,876.16 to € 215,409.60, while lump sum payments were not requested. 29th Annual Report of the Commission on monitoring the application of EU Law (2011), p. 5.

15 Case C-33/90, *Commission v. Italy* [1991] ECR I-5987, para. 24.

### 5.2.3 Member State's Defences

The ECJ has always held a particularly strict approach in assessing Member States' justifications in the context of infringement proceedings. Internal difficulties deriving from, for instance, political, legal or administrative realities within Member States do not have any relevance for the purpose of justifying non-compliance. Similarly, the fact that non-compliance did not cause any damage or was non-intentional does not suffice as justification. Defences based on *force majeure* have furthermore been recognized by the ECJ on extremely rare occasions and under restrictive conditions. This would only be admissible in the presence of external circumstances, independent of the will of the Member State, which make it impossible for it to fulfil its obligations. Such a situation of difficulty must be inevitable, notwithstanding the adoption of all necessary precautions, and even then can only justify the non-conformity during such period as necessary for a diligent administration to remedy it.[16] Moreover, a state cannot justify its failure to comply by alleging a violation by another Member State or by the institutions of their Union law obligations or by alleging the invalidity of the act they arguably violated.[17]

### 5.2.4 The Administrative Procedure

The pre-litigation phase is of fundamental importance in the infringement procedure as a whole. The acts adopted by the Commission in this phase are required to clarify its findings to the national authorities and allow them to put forward their defence in view of possible litigation. At the same time, the exchanges of information that take place in this phase between the national administrations and the Commission are aimed at finding a solution to the alleged violation and avoiding the onset of the case itself. In practice, most contested infringements are in fact resolved during this phase.[18]

The pre-litigation phase commences when a "letter of formal notice" is sent to the Member State in question in accordance with Article 258 TFEU.[19] This letter indicates the alleged infringement(s) and provides a deadline by when the Member State must respond. In practice, such a letter follows an exchange of communication between the Commission and Member State which normally takes the form of informal requests for information, to which the state is obliged to respond in accordance with the obligation of loyal cooperation.[20]

16 Case C-297/08, *Commission v. Italy* [2010] ECR I-1749, para. 85.

17 Case C-404/00, *Commission v. Spain* [2003] ECR I-695, para. 40.

18 A Europe of results. Communication from the Commission, 5.9.2007, COM(2007) 502 final, p. 2.

19 The notion of "letter of formal notice" is not specifically mentioned in the text of the Treaty; it is, in fact, the communication the Commission is obliged to adopt, to give "the State concerned the opportunity to submit its observations" with regard to the supposed charges, as per Art. 258 TFEU.

20 The informal contacts which proceed the formal onset of the infringement proceedings are by now mainly undertaken in the ambit of the so-called EU Pilot, a new system of IT communication between the Commission and the Member States aimed at improving the management of complaints concerning possible violation of Union Law. A Europe of results, p. 5.

When the elements supplied by the state in response to the letter of formal notice are not considered convincing or adequate to justify the closure of the proceedings, the Commission may escalate the procedure by issuing a "reasoned opinion" pursuant to Article 258 TFEU. By this act, the Commission notifies the state of the precise grounds of compliant in a more detailed manner, and in the light of the observations formulated by this state in reply to the letter of formal notice.

The reasoned opinion illustrates the factual and legal elements on which the Commission's allegations are founded. By delimiting the subject-matter of the dispute, this act also supplies the state with the information it requires to defend itself. The reasoned opinion also establishes a deadline within which the interested Member State has to bring the infringement to an end or to present evidence aimed at disputing the Commission's claims.[21]

The Commission does of course have the opportunity to state in the reasoned opinion "the grounds of complaint which it has already made more generally in the letter of formal notice" but cannot introduce new ones. In order to guarantee the rights of defence of the state involved, any new claims can be raised in the ambit of an ongoing infringement procedure only through the adoption of a so-called supplementary letter of formal notice.[22]

If the Member State does not comply with the reasoned opinion within the prescribed deadline or does not present justifications considered sufficient to exclude failure to fulfil, the Commission can start the litigation phase under Article 258(2) TFEU. The Commission is not obliged to bring the matter before the Court on expiration of the deadline indicated in the reasoned opinion, as it is entitled to continue to dialogue with the state involved even after the expiry date if it considers this appropriate, in particular where this could be helpful in bringing an end to the infringement.

## 5.3 The Litigation Phase

### 5.3.1 *Admissibility of the Action and Burden of Proof*

In principle, the fact that a long period of time has elapsed between the adoption of a reasoned opinion and the referral to ECJ does not constitute a condition of inadmissibility of the Commission's action.[23]

The coinciding of the allegations raised by the Commission in the pre-litigation phase and those contained in the application to the Court constitutes a condition of admissibility of

21 In the absence of treaty provisions, both the letter of formal notice and the reasoned opinion usually foresee a deadline of two months for the response. In practice, it is possible for Member States to request the Commission an extension of the said time limit, which if duly motivated, is normally accepted.

22 A supplementary reasoned opinion may also be issued where required to supplement a first reasoned opinion, provided it does not introduce grounds of infringement not present in the letter of formal notice.

23 Case C-297/08, *Commission v. Italy* [2010] ECR I-1749, para. 87.

the action itself. Since the formal letter of notice and the reasoned opinion of the Commission limit the scope of the litigation in question,

> the reasoned opinion and the proceedings brought by the Commission must be based on the same complaints as those set out in the letter of formal notice initiating the pre-litigation procedure in order to guarantee the defence rights of the convened State.[24]

If the Member State has put an end to the infringement after the time limit prescribed by the reasoned opinion there can still be an interest in pursuing the action in order to establish the basis of liability which a Member State may incur, as a result of its default towards other Member States, the Union or private parties.[25]
Generally speaking, it is

> incumbent upon the Commission to prove the infringement alleged by providing the Court with the evidence necessary to enable it to establish that the obligation has not been fulfilled, without being able to rely on any presumption for those purposes.[26]

The Commission might find it difficult to satisfy its burden of proof with regard to cases that raise the problem of the effective transposition by a Member State of the obligations required by a directive. The aforementioned ruling concerning waste disposal in Campania clarified that, in order to prove its allegations, the Commission, which does not have investigative powers on its own, can rely on the elements provided by complainants, public or private bodies, the media, as well as the Member State involved.[27] With regard to the burden of proof charged to the convened State, according to the Court,

> where the Commission has adduced sufficient evidence to establish certain circumstances in the territory of the defendant Member State, it is for that Member State to challenge in substance and in detail the data produced and the inferences drawn.[28]

---

24 Case C-365/97, *Commission v. Italy* [1999] ECR I-781, para. 23.
25 Case C-59/89, *Commission v. Germany* [1991] ECR I-2607, para. 35.
26 Case C-297/08, *Commission v. Italy* [2010] ECR I-1749, para. 101.
27 *Ibid.*, para. 101.
28 *Ibid.*, para. 102.

### 5.3.2 *Content and Effects of the Court's Judgment*

The judgement rendered by the ECJ under Article 258 TFEU has a purely declaratory nature. The Court limits itself to declaring that the convened Member State has failed to fulfil its obligations under Union Law. It cannot however, oblige a state to adopt specific measures, nor has the power to annul or declare void a state measure.
Pursuant to Article 260(1) TFEU, the convened state "shall be required to take the necessary measures to comply with the judgment of the Court". This means, as clarified by the Court, a prohibition having the full force of the law on the competent national authorities against applying a national rule recognized as incompatible with the treaty and, if the circumstances so require, an obligation on them to take all appropriate measure to enable Union law to be fully applied.[29] This obligation arises from the moment in which the judgement is issued and is in force as long as the violation persists.

### 5.3.3 *General and Persistent Infringements*

In a judgment against Ireland concerning waste disposal, the Court admitted that the Commission could bring action not only for individual breaches of Union Law but also for a general and persistent failure to fulfil. The Court noted that when the time limit prescribed by the reasoned opinion expired "Ireland failed to comply, in a general and persistent manner, to its obligations to guarantee the correct implementation of [...] the Directive, tolerating the non-authorized functioning of a large number of waste disposal plants".[30] Following a ECJ judgement which declares such a specific failure to comply, it is not sufficient for the convened state to remedy the infringement specifically objected by the Commission during the proceedings, as the state must also demonstrate that the generalized practice of failure to fulfil a specific obligation has ended. This new case law will likely be developed in the future, especially in the environmental sector where this kind of infringements most frequently occurs.

## 5.4 The Execution of the Court's Judgment

### 5.4.1 *The Role of the Commission*

The Commission also has jurisdiction over the convened State's compliance with the ECJ ruling.[31] Whenever the Commission considers that the state in question has not taken the

29 Case 48/71, *Commission v. Italy* [1972] ECR 529, para. 7.
30 Case C-494/01, *Commission v. Ireland* [2005] ECR I-3430.
31 Irrespective of whether the judgement has been rendered pursuant to Arts. 258(2), 259 or 108(2) TFEU.

measures necessary in order to comply with the judgement, it can again return the matter to the ECJ in order to impose sanctions on the state pursuant to Article 260(2) TFEU.[32] The decision to request to the Court the imposition of the penalty payment comes at the conclusion of a further administrative phase which commences with the adoption by the Commission of a new letter of formal notice against the non-compliant State. Before the changes introduced by the Treaty of Lisbon, this phase was identical to the pre-litigation phase previously described. However, the new Article 260(2) today provides that the Commission is not held to issue another reasoned opinion in order to refer the matter to the ECJ. The Commission's only procedural obligation is to give the non-compliant state the opportunity to present observations. Therefore, it is sufficient for the Commission to notify its observations to the state by means of a new letter of formal notice (pursuant this time to Art. 260 TFEU) to which the state may then submit its own observations. After completion of this obligation, the Commission can bring the matter to the ECJ, specifying as foreseen by the aforementioned provision "the amount of the lump sum or penalty payment to be paid by the Member State concerned which it considers appropriate in the circumstances".[33]

### 5.4.2 *The Type and* Quantum *of the Financial Penalty*

Article 260(2) TFEU provides that whenever the Court "finds that the Member State concerned has not complied with its judgment it may impose a lump sum or penalty payment on it". As explicitly provided by the treaty therefore, the proposals set out by the Commission in the action brought pursuant to Article 260(2) TFEU are not binding for the ECJ;[34] they only constitute a useful point of reference. According to settled case law

> It is for the Court, in each case, in the light of the circumstances of the case before it and the degree of persuasion and deterrence which appears to it to be required, to determine the financial penalties appropriate for making sure that the judgment which previously established the breach is complied with as

32 The possibility of imposing penalty payments on non-compliant Member States was introduced in 1992 by the Treaty of Maastricht; but the first ruling was issued against Greece in 2000.

33 It has been foreseen by the Commission that on the basis of the new procedure provided by Art. 260(2) TFEU, the average duration of the proceedings should be reduced from a period between 12 and 24 months to a period of between 8 and 18 months. Communication from the Commission – Implementation of Art. 260(3) of the Treaty, SEC(2010) 1371 final, para. 3 (OJEU 2011, C 12).

34 An exception to this general principle is provided by Art. 260(3) TFEU which foresees that for "non-com" infringements, the Court may impose the payment of a lump-sum or penalty payment "not exceeding the amount specified by the Commission".

> swiftly as possible and preventing similar infringements of European Union law from recurring.[35]

In the landmark ruling *Commission v. France* of 12 July, 2005, the Court clarified the different purposes pursued by the daily penalty payment and the lump sum penalty, acknowledging for the first time, by reason of the complementarity of the two sanctions, that a state could be simultaneously and cumulatively condemned to pay both.
Imposing only a penalty payment and not also the payment of a lump sum would in fact leave infringements unpunished in those cases that are prolonged following a first judgment and are then remedied by the state just before a second judgement in accordance with Article 260(2) TFEU.[36] This case law has significantly emboldened Member States' efforts to avoid long standing breaches of Union Law. On this point the Court has, however, stated that

> The wording of Article 228 EC [now Art. 260 TFEU] does not indicate [. . .] that an order for the payment of a lump sum should be made automatically, as the Commission contends in the 2005 Communication. By providing that the Court 'may' impose a lump sum payment or a penalty payment on the defaulting Member State, that provision confers a wide discretion upon the Court in deciding whether it is necessary to impose such sanctions.[37]

With regard to the *quantum* of the penalty, the Commission has clarified that it must be calculated on the basis of three fundamental criteria: the seriousness of the infringement, its duration and the necessity to guarantee the dissuasive efficacy of the penalty to avoid recidivism.[38] The seriousness of non-compliance is assessed on the basis of the breached rule at the object of the infringement and the consequences of the breach on general and specific interests. Following the ruling subsequent to Spain's failure to comply with the obligations imposed by the Directive 76/160/EEC, relating to the quality of bathing water, the ECJ has attributed particular relevance to breaches concerning environmental matters.[39] This finding was recently confirmed by the ECJ in two rulings condemning Ireland

---

35 See, Case C-496/09, *Commission v. Italy* [2011] ECR not yet published, paras 36 and 37 as well as, Case C-119/04, *Commission v. Italy* [2006] ECR I-6885, para. 33 and Case C-503/04, *Commission v. Germany* [2007] ECR I-6153.

36 Communication from the Commission, Application of Art. 228 of the EC Treaty [now Art. 260 TFEU] document SEC(2005) 1658, para. 10.1.

37 Case C-121/07, *Commission v. France* [2008] ECR I-9029, para. 63.

38 See Communication from the Commission, Application of Art. 228 of the EC Treaty [now Art. 260 TFEU], recently updated by Communication SEC(2010) 923, Application of Art. 260 of the Treaty on the Functioning of the EU. Updating of data used to calculate lump sum and penalty payments to be proposed by the Commission to the Court of Justice in infringement proceedings.

39 Case C-278/01, *Commission v. Spain* [2003] ECR I-4141, para. 57.

to financial sanctions[40] for the prolonged infringement of Directive 85/337/EEC on the assessment of projects on the environment[41] and of Directive 75/442/EEC on waste[42] respectively.

The Commission has clarified that, in assessing the general consequences of an infringement, it would assess whether this leads to serious or irreparable damage to the health of human beings or to the environment.[43] When formulating its request for penalties, the Commission therefore performs a mathematical calculation based on its own pre-defined parameters. The Court, however, seems to determine the amount of penalties without disclosing any calculation, and seemingly more on the basis of equitable considerations. Factors taken into consideration by the Court in deciding whether to condemn the state to the payment of a lump sum may include the legal and factual context of the infringement, whether the state has previously breached the same rule, the lack of tangible initiatives aimed at solving the breach in the period between the first and second ruling and the level of difficulty of the transposition.[44]

### 5.4.3 *Duration of the Penalty*

The condemned state is held to the payment of the penalty from the date on which the ECJ judgement is pronounced and for the duration of the period in which the infringement persists. Union law does not lay down any specific provision regarding the settlement of disputes that may arise between a Member State and the Commission on the occasion of the enforcement of such a judgment, however, the General Court has recently held that Commission is responsible for recovering the amounts that would be due to the budget of the EU pursuant to a judgment of the ECJ imposing sanctions on Member States.

The General Court further clarified that in the context of enforcing a judgment of the ECJ imposing a penalty payment on a Member State, the Commission must be able to assess the measures adopted by the Member State to comply with the judgment in order, *inter alia*, to prevent the Member State which has failed to fulfil its obligations from simply

40 Respectively, Case C-279/11, *Commission v. Ireland* [2012], not yet published and Case C-374/11, *Commission v. Ireland* [2012], not yet published.

41 Council Directive 85/337/EEC of 27 June 1985 on the assessment of the effects of certain public and private projects on the environment (OJ 1985 L 175, p. 40), as amended by Council Directive 97/11/EC of 3 March 1997 (OJ 1997 L 73, p. 5).

42 Council Directive 75/442/EEC of 15 July 1975 on waste (OJ 1975 L 194, p. 39), as amended by Council Directive 91/156/EEC of 18 March 1991 (OJ 1991 L 78, p. 32).

43 Communication from the Commission, Application of Art. 228 of the EC Treaty [now Art. 260 TFEU], para. 16.4.

44 In the above mentioned judgements against Ireland (footnote 40), for the purpose of establishing financial penalties, the ECJ took into account the fact that Ireland's ability to pay had been diminished as a result of the economic crisis.

taking measures that, in reality, have the same content as those that were the subject of the judgment of the ECJ. However, the exercise of that power of appraisal can prejudice neither the rights – and in particular the procedural rights – of the Member States, as they result from the procedure set out in Article 258 TFEU, nor the exclusive jurisdiction of the ECJ to rule on the compliance of national legislation with Union law.[45]

## 5.5 Conclusions

The acceleration provided by the Treaty of Lisbon under the new Articles 260(3) TFEU and 260(2) TFEU concerning "non-com" cases and the request for penalty payments respectively, together with the ECJ case law on the "general and persistent infringements" constitute new elements which render the infringement proceeding an even more incisive tool to ensure the compliance of the Member States with their obligations deriving from Union Law.

Furthermore, the Commission has now held for some time that "priority should be attached to those infringements which present the greatest risks, widespread impact for citizens".[46]

When considering that European *acquis* in the environmental sector is mostly composed of directives,[47] and that the violations in this sector are among those most likely to have a negative impact on citizens, it is easy to foresee that in the future the Commission will continue to pursue infringements concerning environmental matters in a even more rapid and more attentive way.

## References

R. Adam & A. Tizzano, *Lineamenti di diritto dell'Unione europea* (2nd edn), Torino, 2010.

M. Condinanzi & R. Mastroianni, *Il contenzioso dell'Unione europea*, Torino, 2009.

---

45 Case T-33/09, *Portugal v. Commission* [2011] not yet published paras 81 and 82. On the basis of these considerations, the General Court annulled the Commission decision, ruling that the Commission was not entitled to decide, in the context of the enforcement of a judgement pursuant to Art. 260(2) TFEU, that a new law adopted by Portugal did not comply with Union law and then draw conclusions from this for the calculation of the penalty payment determined by the ECJ. In so far as it considered that the system of rules introduced by that law did not constitute a correct transposition of Union law, the Commission should have initiated new infringement proceedings. An appeal against this judgement is currently pending before the ECJ (Case C-292/11P). On the same subject, but with an opposite result, see also Case T-139/06, *France v. Commission* [2011], not yet published.

46 A Europe of results. Communication of the Commission, p. 5.

47 Communication of the Commission on implementing European Community Environmental Law, COM (2008) 773 final, p. 8.

A. Dashwood, M. Dougan, B. Rodger, E. Spaventa & D. Wyatt, *Wyatt and Dashwood's European Union Law*, Oxford, 2011.

G. Gaja & A. Adinolfi, *Introduzione al diritto dell'Unione europea*, Bari-Rome, 2010.

I. Kilbey, 'Financial Penalties under Article 228(2) EC: Excessive Complexity?', 44 *Common Market Law Review*, 2007, pp. 743-759.

K. Lenaerts, 'The Rule of Law and the Coherence of the Judicial System of the European Union', 44 *Common Market Law Review*, 2007, pp. 1625-1659.

P. Mori, *Articoli 226-228, in* A. Tizzano (Ed.), *Trattati dell'Unione europea e della Comunità europea*, Milan, 2005, pp. 1057-1071.

L. Prete & B. Smulders, 'The Coming Age of Infringement Proceedings', 47 *Common Market Law Review*, 2010, pp. 9-61.

P. Wennerås, 'A New Dawn for Commission Enforcement under Articles 226 and 228 EC: General and Persistent (GAP) Infringements, Lump Sums and Penalty Payments', 43 *Common Market Law Review*, 2006, pp. 31-61.

# 6 Court of Justice's Rulings Against Italy Relating to Infringements of EU Environmental Law

*Andrea Guazzarotti*

## 6.1 Infringement Proceedings

Firstly, it must be pointed out that Italy succeeded in reducing the number of cases under consideration by 50% between 2006 and 2011 (with a reduction of approximately 15% since 2010).[1] Different types of infringement proceedings in this field need to be considered: in addition to the "normal" infringement proceeding arising from incorrect implementation or violation of European Union (EU) Directives there is also the proceeding for failure to transpose the directives. This differs from the 'normal' one in so far as litigation can be initiated more quickly and almost automatically by the Commission;[2] for this procedure, the Lisbon Treaty has given the Commission additional power: that of being able to request the application of financial penalties during the first referral for non-compliance (in other cases these penalties can only be applied in the event of a second referral for "non-fulfilment" at the first ruling of the Court of Justice which determined an infringement pursuant to Article 260(2) TFEU).[3] In addition to this, there is the execution phase of the ruling: a procedure which can be launched by the Commission whenever a Member State has failed to implement adequate measures to comply with the

1 See Note prot. DCPC 273 P - 2.36.4.19 [2011] issued by the Department for European Policies at the Presidency of the Council of Ministers concerning infringement proceedings against Italy in the course of the year 2010.

2 In the event of non-compliance within the prescribed period, the Commission "automatically" issues a formal letter of notice to the States which have failed to forward their transposition procedures. When no adequate response is forwarded by the state in question, the Commission can avail itself of the right to appeal to the Court without delay (approximately nine months from the issue of letter of notice). In the case of persisting state inertia in the presence of a reasoned opinion, the state shall not be entitled to present appeal (persistent non-compliance by the state automatically results in a sentence of culpability from the Court). In such cases, the Commission, namely in the event of failure to transpose, only adopts cautionary policies wherein the phenomenon involves a large number of states, which suggests the objective difficulty in the transposition of the Directive at issue. See R. Adam, seminary presentation *Non compliance in Italy: Infringement proceedings with regard to environmental matters* University of Macerata, 2011.

3 The Commission, by bringing an action for infringement under Art. 258 TFEU, may ask, "when it deems appropriate", the payment of the lump sum or penalty if "the Member State concerned has failed to fulfill its obligation to notify measures transposing a directive adopted under a legislative procedure" (Art. 260(3) TFEU).

ruling of the Court. If the Commission finds that an infringement exists, it may impose a lump sum payment or a penalty payment to be applied by the Court.[4] In such procedures, the Commission sends a letter of formal notice and is under no obligation to supply reasoned opinion (Art. 260(2) TFEU, which has in this way simplified and speeded up procedures prior to the Treaty of Lisbon).

It is important to bear in mind that infringement proceedings (and possible sanctions) against Italy should be classified under three distinct headings. Proceedings for non-transposition, can lead to financial sanctions (which once the action has been started, will almost certainly be applied, even where the state complies late or rather after the action has been lodged, the so-called lump sums). Further to this, they represent a more relevant and radical malfunction of the national legal system. Showing a certain amount of concern, the Note issued by the Department for European Policies, (hereafter: the Note) shows how an increase in the number of proceedings for non-transposition, rose from 29 to 34 cases between 2009-2010 (11 of which related to transposition by means of legislative act and a surprising 23 related to secondary legislation or administrative acts which cannot invoke the political complexities and lengthy of legislative procedures).[5] Furthermore, the Note shows a worrying tendency in the increase of infringement proceedings for failure to apply the previous rulings on account of the other risk of serious penalty payments.[6]

With regard to the "material" classification of infringement proceedings against Italy, the environment still holds the negative record for the number of proceedings while proceedings in other fields are on the increase.[7]

Environmental issues are those with the greatest number of proceedings which involve the regions, particularly regarding waste management,a highly technical and complex area.[8]

The environmental field remains therefore the most at risk of procedures resulting in penalty payments. A further consideration must be made here in relation to the latter. Serious penalty payments for infringements, much more likely since the Lisbon Treaty,

4 Prete-Smulders 2010, pp. 49 *et seq.*; Kilbey 2007, pp. 743 *et seq.*

5 The Note clearly shows how the phenomenon imposes the need for an increased sense of responsibility to the Administration bodies involved in the transposition procedures, in particular Administrations which have been involved at a UE level in drawing up formal documentation. In 2010 the number of non-compliance actions (also taking into account their classification) has multiplied by four to one, confirming a "structural lateness in compliance mechanisms". At this point (January 2012) there are four cases of environmental non-compliance still open.

6 This Note regards 11 procedures (January 2011), one of which has already finished with a final and irrevocable Court decision (C-99/02; C-496/09), at this point (January 2012) there are still 10 cases open, 7 of which are concerned with environmental issues.

7 Environmental issues, 32 cases; health issues, 19; fiscal and customs issues, 17; transport, 17; work and welfare issues 10. At this point (January 2012) 33 environmental cases are open but 3 of these have already been judged: C-50/10; C-491/08; C-508/09.

8 The Note clearly shows how infringement proceedings applied to the regions in the environmental field continue to fluctuate at around 70% while those relating to other sectors have decreased.

cannot remediate the serious damage caused to the environment by an inadequate national or local policy which is in conflict with EU legislation, however, they could have the positive deterrent effect of discouraging such policies, ex ante, enforcing the EU mechanisms of control and penalty payment in a sector always affected by the scarce effectiveness of EU law.[9] Even where the risk of financial sanctions has not led to an improvement in the national policy, (especially, in terms of strengthening those authorities responsible for environmental protection), it is clear that the structural deficit in our country can only worsen as a result of relevant penalty payments (decimating state financial resources in an indiscriminate way without the provision of new funds for administrations and/or environmental policies).[10]

A further characteristic related to environmental issues is the infringement proceedings regarding "general and persistent" violations of EU legislation. This is a new approach which has no formal basis in treaties.[11] Subsequent to the first Court ruling on environmental matters issued in 2005, Italy was sentenced to further penalties on more than one occasion (see *infra*). Standard practice appears to show great potential in terms of controlling the States. This point will be highlighted later along with the ruling related to Italy; however, it should be mentioned here that we are faced with the emergence of a kind of "state administration" by the Commission in certain fields, given that the Commission has the power to demand explanation from the state on how the problematic sectors are managed for many years following the first Court ruling, without it ever becoming clear when the infringement proceeding under Article 260 may close since every new fact may result in proceeding being reopened with immediate referral to the Court.[12]

## 6.2 Environmental Litigation: A Preliminary Framework

With regard to Court rulings against Italy relating to environmental infringements in the period in question (2000-2011), these can be put into various categories. Most importantly, the 37 cases under consideration are almost all condemnations with very few exceptions. It is therefore apparent that the Commission only refers the most flagrant violations of EU law.

It is also apparent that the sentence represents nothing more than an additional prelitigation "phase" which seems aimed not so much as at resolving the dispute linked to the different ways of interpreting the legal provisions from which EU obligations

9 Wennerås 2007.

10 The Commission DG is well aware of the problem and delayed commencing "second degree" infringement proceedings under Art. 260(2) TFEU with regard to a failure to comply or unsatisfactory compliance with the Court ruling concerning waste disposal in Campania (C-297/08 [2010] (Adam 2011).

11 Wennerås 2006.

12 Adam 2011.

are derived rather than to "induce the *State to fulfil* these legal obligations". The Commission attempts to resolve the problems relating to unsatisfactory or scarce implementation of EU legislation in the preliminary phase of infringements, favouring an informal/communicative approach and only threatens a referral to the Court of Justice as a *last resort.*[13]

When no result is achieved at this phase, the Commission tries to obtain the first ruling (even when legal aspects are undisputed, as long as the defendant state often recognizes its own responsibility in the pre-litigation phase, and at times, also in the litigation phase). The first ruling can be exploited by the Commission to exert pressure on the state by implying the threat of inevitable penalty payments with the second ruling, *ex* Article 260 (2) TFEU.

Of the 37 sentences under consideration, the majority (16) involve bad application cases, followed by sentences of non-conformity of national legislation (14), finally, those sentences concerning the non-transposition of Directives (7). This corresponds to a more or less global tendency in environmental matters. The Commission's most recent report on the implementation of community environmental legislation among all States (relating to 2005, published in 2006),[14] revealed 576 bad application cases, 98 of non-conformity cases, 124 cases of non-transposition (or the non-communication of transposition measures).

For Italy the most important sectors from a quantitative and qualitative point of view are those relating to the waste disposal sector (12) where the only "general and persistent infringement" was ruled (C-135/05), as well as the ruling regarding the serious situation of urban refuse in Campania, and the sentence concerning "urban refuse awareness" established by the Italian legislator in contrast with directives (C-263/05, C-194/05, C-195/05). Other issues under examination include the conservation of local wildlife in its natural habitat (9); the protection of water and treatment of urban sewage within the European framework (5); the field of air quality, gaseous emissions and pollution (6); lastly, the field of environmental impact assessment (EIA) which can be included with the case relating to the non-transposition of Directives in terms of public participation in the elaboration of plans and programmes (4). With regard to the latter "transversal" matter, related to procedures aimed at reducing environmental damage provoked by man, (be it in a public or private capacity), it is evident that various infringements in the field of natural habitat conservation have resulted from the inadequate compliance with EIA (such as Case C-304/05 concerning the ski slopes in the Stelvio National park; Case C-491/08 concerning the "Is Arena" tourist resort which involves a natural site of Community importance in Sardinia; Case C-388/05, concerning the realization of an

13 According to the Commission, the judicial review "is not the only nor the most efficient means to guarantee compliance (with community law)": *Implementation of EU Environmental Law: Survey Highlights Serious Shortcomings*, IP/04/1038, Brussels [2004]. Andersen 2008, p. 156 and p. 166.

14 *See* The 7th annual report on the implementation and application of Community environmental law 2005, SEC(2006) 1143 [2006].

industrial zone within the special protection zone "Steppes and Valleys in the Gargano Region": see *infra*).

With regard to the sharing of responsibility among the State, the regions and local authorities for such rulings, things become a little more complex. Given the inextricable nature of legislative and especially administrative functions, when reading the ruling, it is not always easy to understand what the unique or main cause for the infringement is. Apart from simple cases in which the responsibility of the region is clear (such as the case of regional legislation giving specific dispensations to the Directives on the conservation of wild birds: C-164/09, C-503/06, C-508/09; or projects concerning regional public works performed without adopting EIA: C-87/02), or to local authorities (such as the cases of purifiers in the municipality of Milan and the Province of Varese: C-396/00 and C-293/05), there are many cases in which state and territorial responsibility are presumed equal, excluding the possibility of an attribution of prevalent responsibility to either. Cases of non-transposition which are apparently attributable exclusively to the State, could reveal traces of joint regional responsibility (*see* Cases C-22/02 and C-348/02, in which the Government justifies the delay based on the need for *national legislation concerning* the transposition of the Directives to be worked on with the regions). In this context, it is also interesting to note a case where the non-implementation was entirely local (such as the construction of the "third alternative" to the Brescia urban waste incinerator) and at first sight would seem to be attributable to poor administrative implementation by the local authorities while it actually turned out to be a failure to correctly apply the national law which governed the implementation of the EU laws in the sector (C-255/05). Of equal importance in the sharing of responsibilities is the region's lack of providing technical data relative to the location of hydro-graphic basins, where state defence invokes late intervention justified by regional bureaucratic delays (C-85/07, C-127/99). Another relevant case is that concerning the failure to develop and implement waste reception and handling plans for all Italian ports (C-368/07): Responsibility for compliance with the legislation related to ports is shared by the state and the region (Art. 117(3) Italian Constitution), but constitutional Court's jurisprudence has always differentiated between two categories of ports depending on whether the ports are of national or local importance. As a consequence, different responsibility for the same proceedings relating to one EU obligation may arise.

## 6.3 INFRINGEMENT PROCEEDINGS AS A MOTIVATOR

An observation can be connected to the cases mentioned in the previous chapter regarding infringement proceedings between central and local governments. Following the analysis of some cases, it emerges that the infringement has the role of supporting central government in order to induce local governments to adopt policies which had been previously unwelcomed or simply ignored.

The case of the Milan purification plants is emblematic where during the pre-litigation phase, the government had first communicated to the Commission that three purification plants had been planned, and then declared a state of emergency in order to start a fast-track procedure for the construction of such plants through a state commissioner ad acta (C-396/00 and C-293/05). The case can be interpreted as a manifestation of the inefficiency of government control on local non-compliance as well as a strategy based on emergency logic deriving from the same infringement procedure, as if the government wishes for strong European intervention to goad them into imposing the realization of public works on a local level. Moreover, in some cases the outcomes of pre-litigation procedures show how central government succeeds in imposing compliance to European legislation on regions and local authorities which had not so far been requested or obtained.[15]

The role played by infringement proceedings in goading the State (but also regions and local authorities) into activating environmental policies otherwise ignored has already been mentioned.[16] A passage of one of the analyzed cases is highly clarifying: rejecting the state objection on the extremely brief time conceded by the Commission in the reasoned opinion, the Court argued that the Italian Republic had already had a six-year period in which to comply from the time limit of transposition fixed in the Directive to that prescribed in the reasoned opinion (Case C-293/05, para. 25). This is like an attempt to stigmatize the attitude of the state which seems to misinterpret the time limit for the implementation of impositions set out in a Directive, making out that the time limit starts from the moment of the statement of reasoned opinion and not from the time limit set by the Directive itself. To this regard, there are many cases in which the government has pleaded delayed compliance, after the expiration of the time limit established in the reasoned opinion (see Cases C-122/05, C-394/05, C-313/06, C-69/07, C-491/08, C-503/06 and C-164/09). The Court usually refuses to take into consideration such delayed compliance, on the basis of Article 258 TFUE (former Art. 226 TEC), sustaining that the state did not comply within the prescribed time limits. In similar cases, it is evident that the Commission had a different view point from that of the government with regard to the acceptance of late interventions (otherwise they would have renounced the referral). Before the Court, the Italian Government contested the Commission's point of view, sustaining that it had already made amends to the infringement under consideration before the referral procedure. The Court ignored the late intervention of the Government condemning Italy for its non-compliance

15 See Case C-368/07, *supra* para. 2, with regard to the non-compliance of waste disposal dispositions relating to ports where over a period of 16,5 months the government managed to forward to the Commission information on important ports, such as Naples, Ravenna, Genova, Gioia Tauro, Livorno and Taranto. The procedures regarding hunting dispensations relating to obligations under the Directive regarding "Birds" (C-164/09, C-503/06) show clear pressure from the state leading to new legislation aimed at compliance with EU legislation (C-503/06).

16 Prete & Smulders 2010, p. 14.

within the time limits, leaving doubts with regard to the effectiveness of such intervention. This will eventually give rise to new consideration for a related procedure under Article 260 TFEU (former Article 228 TEC), concerning failure to comply to the preliminary Court ruling, wherein the state is held under "special surveillance".

## 6.4 The Effectiveness of Infringement Proceedings in Environmental Matters

When considering the effectiveness of infringement proceedings, it is important to underline that only two interim and precautionary measures were issued by the Court, in which Italy was ordered to suspend the application of laws that were suspected to have violated EU legislation (both cases related to regional hunting laws in which dispensations were issued in contrast to the prohibitions set out in Directive 79/409/CEE).[17] However, cases still exist in which the absence of adequate precautionary measures aimed at the prevention of irreversible damage to the environment occur (considering that the pre-litigation stage lasts an average of 26 months). While it is true that the introduction of precautionary measures in the litigation stage would undoubtedly mean a reform of the treaty,[18] it is also true that the adoption of precautionary measures by the Court during the litigation stage is much more limited during infringement proceedings than in others proceedings [Prete & Smulders 2010, p. 40]. This proves to be a weak point of infringement proceedings in environmental issues, wherein the Commission limits itself to defining the appropriate priority criteria to be adopted when starting infringement procedures, namely the irreversible damage.[19]

Emblematic examples of similar ineffectiveness of the procedures are to be found in the cases examined. The cases involved concern mainly public or private civil work projects that have been approved without having undergone an EIA (or similar preliminary assessments), wherein the first Court ruling was issued after the total or partial realization of the project, and where environmental damage had been sufficiently proved (see Cases C-87/02, C-388/05 and C-304/05). Moreover, the question is: what can a Court ruling do in such cases compared to the irreversible damage caused to the habitat; the same can be said for a possible negative ruling in the execution phase of the sentence which results in financial penalties (Art. 260 TFUE): it seems that the Commission cannot demand States to make amends by providing for the destruction of completed civil works realized in compliance with national legislation not in line with EU Directives.

---

17 Court order dated 10.12.2009 (C-573/08 R); court order dated 19.12.2006 (C-503/06 R).

18 Wennerås 2007, pp. 260 *et seq.*

19 See *Commission communication related to the transposition of EU environmental legislation,* COM(2008) 773

An interesting case is that of the realization of a tourist centre with a golf course in a site of Community importance in Sardinia called "Is Arenas" (C-491/08). The site, which is protected on a Community (now EU) level, became the object of an agreement between building contractors, local authority and the region for the realization of a tourist resort in 1997. The letter of formal notice from the Commission was received in April 2000, after construction of the golf course in the centre had been completed; the Commission did not however induce the territorial Authority to revoke the building project which proceeded to final completion. Subsequently, reasoned opinion was given in February 2001 followed by two formal letters of notice in December 2004 and December 2005 neither of which were adequately addressed by government measures; the last and most decisive reasoned opinion arrived in February 2008 (with no answer by the government). In the litigation stage, the Government (which clearly did not want to or could not impose itself upon the region, even though it would have been able to avail itself of substituting powers with regard to Community obligations, under Art. 120(2) It. Const.) recognizes the impracticality of its previous proposals for the reduction of protected areas, and announced yet another modification to the original project in an attempt to avoid an adverse ruling (July 2010).
The aforementioned case shows clearly how the state (especially where "infrastructural" political bodies such as regions and local authorities are involved) bide their time with the Commission, turning to mild recommendations only after the presentation of the referral, although nothing was done in terms of environmental conservation during the prolonged pre-litigation stage. This case is emblematic of the highest grade of ineffectiveness and weakness of the infringement proceedings wherein local authorities are involved rather than central government. Some important results have been achieved in this field through the practice of the so-called "package meetings", aimed at strengthening intermediate political bodies involved in the infringement proceeding. While previously the Commission limited itself to dialogue with the state, the state limited itself to forwarding the findings to the territorial bodies involved, these "package meetings" (usually held in the capital city of the state in question) involve central government and territorial representatives as well as European Commission members. The presence of Commission representatives has the beneficial effect of giving local government key figures involved more responsibility, highlighting violations of Union laws when these findings are conveyed directly to the Commission without passing through central Government. Evidence of such standard procedures came to light in only one of the cases under review (Case C-297/08 [2010] para. 25), related to the well-known and serious refuse disposal issue in Campania. The outcome of such standard procedures seems to have yielded positive results so far, with a considerable reduction in the opening of infringement proceedings against Italy.[20]

20 Adam 2011.

## 6.5 "General and Persistent Infringements"

With regard to the increased effectiveness of Commission surveillance on States in the field of environmental protection and in particular on Italy, a new approach to the infringement procedures has already been referred to as "general and persistent" (a procedure which began with the so-called *Irish Waste* case, C-494/01, *Commission v. Ireland* [2005], and subsequently applied to Italy in Case C-135/05 related to the illegal dumping of waste). The standard procedure is part of a strategic Commission plan aimed at rationalising the use of infringement proceedings, grouping related cases in the same sector and implementing horizontal procedures with the aim of solving systematic problems of bad application or non-compliance.[21] The main advantage to the effectiveness of the procedure is that one single act of compliance within the time limit will not prove that the state has fulfilled its duty as laid down in the reasoned opinion, *i.e.* will not prove that the structural problem at issue has been resolved. A further strategic advantage is that the Commission has the power to enforce its own decision also through cases ascertained *after* the statement of reasoned opinion: this does not involve an inappropriate extension of the underlying cause of action but the generalized and persistent nature of the infringement. Furthermore, the fundamental advantage for the Commission is the possibility to impose the burden of proof on the State, whereby it is the responsibility of the national government to demonstrate that the series of cases in question represent isolated incidents and not a generalized and persistent practice of infringement of EU legislation. Moreover, subsequent to the first ruling concerning general and persistent infringements, it will no longer be sufficient for the state to solve individual cases in order to avoid a second adverse ruling under Article 260 and thus financial penalties for non-compliance with the first ruling. On the contrary, the state must provide for the prevention of further cases (such as the illegal dumping of waste) as each one of these cases represents the persistence of the original structural problem.[22]

With regard to this general framework, it is interesting to analyze in depth the reply of the Italian government in the first case of *generalized and persistent infringement* (Case C-135/05, *supra*). In the formal letter of notice dated July 2003, the Commission did not receive any useful information, while in the reasoned opinion dated December 2003, the Commission received no reply from the Italian Government at all, which was clearly uncomfortable with the new standard procedure involved.

Moreover, in the litigation phase, the Government objected to the inadmissibility of the referral, pleading that the vagueness and indeterminacy of the case prevented the rapid preparation of a defence. The Commission replied sustaining its right to examine the question of waste disposal throughout Italy in a single legal process, depending on the

21 See 7th yearly Report; as well as Communication COM(2008) 773, *supra*.

22 Wennerås 2007, pp. 266 *et seq.*

most suitable solution to correct structural problems in connection with the alleged non-compliance (paras 18 *et seq.*). The Court found in favour of the Commission, ruling that

> where the Commission relies on detailed complaints revealing repeated failures to comply with the provisions of the directive, it is incumbent on the Member State concerned to contest specifically the facts alleged in those complaints. Likewise, where the Commission has adduced sufficient evidence to show that a Member State's authorities have developed a repeated and persistent practice which is contrary to the provisions of a directive, it is incumbent on that Member State to challenge in substance and in detail the information produced and the consequences flowing therefrom ( . . . ).

That obligation rests on the Member States under the duty of genuine cooperation, enshrined in Article 10 EC, throughout the procedure provided for by Article 226 EC. It is apparent from the case-file that the Italian authorities did not fully cooperate with the Commission for the purposes of the investigation of the present case at the stage of the pre-litigation procedure (*ibid.*, para. 32).

## 6.6 Conclusions

If we wanted to find common denominator that characterize these ten years of litigation concerning Italy in the field of environmental issues, it could be said that case records show a number of "critical" points, within which, probably at the core, there is a clear cultural *deficit failure* of the Italian authorities (and Italian society) in terms of environmental protection.

As we have already mentioned, the majority of negative rulings have been in the field of waste disposal where the worst non-compliances of EU Directives regarding environment have been found. The case of waste disposal in Campania is obviously the most serious (Case C-297/08). This case has a series of local peculiarities (in primis, the problem of organized crime) that may not allow for generalizations.[23] One generalization which could be applied however is probably that of the logic of emergency and occasional intervention, decided by central government only when the "disease" reaches an apex and after having neglected the local management of refuse for a long period of time. What may be more interesting however are the cases of parochial interpretation of the concept of waste disposal management which are among those rare cases where legal argument of some depth

23 Note that, after the Court decision, the European Court of Human Rights condemned Italy in the Campania waste disposal issue, referring to precedents in Luxembourg which exclude justification owing to circumstances beyond the State's control as in the case of *Di Sarno and others v. Italy* [2012] (para. 111).

are put forward by the Italian defence (Cases C-486/04, C-263/05, C-195/05, C-194/05, C-270/03).

The existence of structural (and cultural) difficulties for the political bodies to impose the internalization of an environmental issue upon public and private bodies which requires an adequate public control structure and relative competent managerial staff is evident (see Case C-270/03). In certain cases, this concerns a truly "conflict of interest" within centralised political power which clearly demonstrates interests conflicting with environment when supporting ambitious programmes of civil works aimed at economic growth.[24]

Another field in which there is a deep discrepancy between national and European environmental culture, is that relating to the environmental impact assessment (and similar). It is not just the number of cases involved which is striking (Cases C-304/05, C-255/05, C-40/07, C-87/02, C-83/03, C-388/05, C-486/04), but also the will of the state to defend itself against complaints in the pre-litigation stage and during litigation, citing the ability to make amends for the infringement of environmental law through an *a posteriori* assessment performed by the same political bodies (or by not independent technical bodies) who authorized civil work projects (public or private) with a presumed environmental impact under EU Legislation (see Cases C-304/05 and C-255/05).

## References

S. Andersen, 'Procedural Overview and Substantive Comments on Articles 226 and 228 EC', 27 *Yearbook of European Law*, 1, 2008, pp. 121-166.

I. Kilbey, 'Financial Penalties under Article 228(2) EC: Excessive Complexity?', 44 *Common Market Law Review* 3, 2007, pp. 743-759.

L. Prete & B. Smulders, 'The Coming of Age of Infringement Proceedings', 47 *Common Market Law Review* 1, 2010, pp. 9-61.

P. Wennerås, 'A New Dawn for Commission Enforcement under Articles 226 and 228 EC: General and Persistent (GAP) Infringements, Lump Sums and Penalty Payments', 43 *Common Market Law Review* 1, 2006, pp. 3-62.

P. Wennerås, *The Enforcement of EC Environmental Law*, New York, 2007.

24 *See* Case C-194/05 (paras 28 *et seq.*), where the Italian government underlines the relationship existing between the controversial provisions and the realization of a vast civil works project relating to the country's infrastructures for which the excavation of soil and rock (excluded from the Community's concept of waste, expecting its reutilization) is indispensable.

# 7 Non-Compliance with European Environmental Law: Evidence from Case Study

*Erik Longo and Claudia Pennacchietti**

## 7.1 Introduction

This chapter examines the causes of failure of Member States to comply with European environmental laws through the analysis of some infringement proceedings that have been opened against Italy. The thesis developed in these pages is that, through many cases, such lack of compliance derives from the misuse of harmonization tools made available at European level.

The first part of this chapter is dedicated to several cases of non-compliance of Italian regulation against with European directives; the second is dedicated to the analysis of some problems arising from such infringement procedures and the development of the aforementioned thesis.

## 7.2 Five Cases of Non-Compliance with Environmental Directives

Starting from infringement procedures, we will analyze some cases of *mis-implementation* of EU directives within the Italian legal system. Such a approach will consent us to examine more closely the problems underlying dynamics of non-compliance of Italian laws against EU directives. To this aim, we will also consider the Court of Justice's proof of Italy's responsibility for the failure to comply.[1] We have collected and analyzed a large number of cases of infringement within the Italian laws and then ranked them depending on the gravity of the infringement. Data collection criteria considered issues of the transposition process at legislation and at administration level. The cases under examination

* The authors would like to thank the Chief of Department for European Policies at the Prime Minister's Office of the Italian Republic, Prof. Roberto Adam and Dr. Caterina Gestri for the precious support during the research. The chapter was finalized on 27 January 2012.

* Although the chapter is the result of a shared work effort by the two authors, Claudia Pennacchietti is responsible for the writing of Sections 7.2.4, 7. 2.5, 7.3 and 7.3.1, Erik Longo edited the remaining Sections.

1 According to the Art. 258 TFEU a judgment of the ECJ declaring a failure of a Member State to fulfil a Treaty obligation is declaratory in nature. The defaulting Member State is required to take all necessary measures to comply with that judgment within the shortest possible period.

relate to five macro-sectors of the European environmental policies: *waste*, *water* conservation, *wild life* protection, *air* quality and *environmental risk* control.

### *7.2.1 Waste Legislation*

Over the past decade, Italy has been subject to various sanctions by the Court of Justice due to its inadequacy to implement of the so-called "waste framework directive" (75/442/CEE).[2]

The most relevant sanctions have been registered during 2004. Among all procedures opened, the Case C-135/05, deserves a particular mention. In this case the European Court of Justice (ECJ) has already issued a sentence of sanctions concerning Italy.[3] There are two main reasons for this procedure worth to be considered. First, unlike previous cases, the Commission acted on the basis of a so-called "horizontal approach": the question of the disposal of refuse in all Italian territory was examined within a sole procedure. It is a serious and widespread violation: the data collected by the Commission has been used to highlight the existence of numerous illegal dumps, sites of abandoned waste, the dumping of unauthorized waste and non-specified sites, some of which containing dangerous waste. Secondly, the ruling of the ECJ reveals the existence of a serious of "responsibility for non-compliance". The issue could be summarized as follows: in a situation of generalized non-compliance attributable to administrations charged with the implementation of reception rules of the European directives, could the responsibility of the non-compliance itself be attributed only to these authorities, or is it also necessary to look at the legislation itself to understand if the origin of the administrative non-compliance lies there? As can be seen, it involves an issue which is anything but linear. However, it would be too simple to limit oneself to declaring that in a complex process the course of a failure must lead back to a single territorial level responsible for the implementation of the environmental measures. In the ruling, the Court clarifies the problem, indicating an approach concerning the internal administrative practice within which a deeper problem connected to the incorrect reception of rules can be traced. The Court's decision contains three fundamental opinions: a) the public legislator can decide how to comply with the measures and competences implemented by a European resolution within its own legal system notwithstanding the respect of the aims of the latter; b) the choice to attribute the execution on an administrative level means that the eventual non-implementation is without doubt attributed to the latter; c) however, this does not mean that such a charge is exclusive because the "non-compliance to the EU rules" can reveal itself to be a flaw in

2 Directive implemented in Italy by the Delegated Decree, 5 February 1997, n. 22 (so-called "Decreto Ronchi").

3 Case C-135/05, *Commission of the European Communities v. Italian Republic* [2007] ECR I-3475 (Infringement proceeding No. 2003/2077).

the legislator's choice of methods, which in the Court's opinion results is an abuse of the discretion awarded by the European law.[4]

A further and exemplary case the matter of implementation difficulty concerns the "waste management emergency" in the Campania Region.[5] In the relative infringement proceeding, the dynamics of the relationship between the European Commission and Italy are observed, where the inflexibility of the first contrasts with the inefficacy of action of the authorities of the second, not always compliant with harmonization procedures foreseen in the directive. This is not the right place either to go too deep into details of the issue or to find the causes or the attempts of resolution conducted by the national governments, nor to look at the problems of administrative mismanagement that led to an attempted resolution through the creation of extraordinary authorities with exceptional powers. However, we report some fundamental steps, which could be useful for the examination being conducted. Above all, it is essential to remember that the issue began to have formal relevance for the EU in the first half of 2007, corresponding with the waste collection crisis in the City of Naples, when the Commission decided to send a letter of formal notice to the Italian government (29 June 2007) notifying the non-compliance with Articles 4 and 5 of the Directive 2006/12/EC.[6] The core of the charges was based on the absence of an adequate integrated network of waste treatment in Campania, which could have radically eliminated the continuous on-going situation of emergency. In the letter, the European Commission conceded a period of one month from reception of the letter for Italy to present its observations. After an unsatisfactory answer from the Italian Government to the first letter, on 17 October 2007, the Commission decided to send a subsequent letter of formal notice in which it underlined the terms of the dispute for the non-implementation of the directives concerning waste requested the submission of observations within 60 days from the reception and made the adoption of a new management plan for waste in the Campania Region the condition for the installation of an efficient waste collection, treatment and disposal system. In the absence of a solution to the serious emergency situation and the inadequacy of the Italian government's letter of reply, the Commission sent (31 January 2008) a reasoned opinion after reception of a further answer sent by the Italian State, the Commission decided to defer Italy to the Court for non-compliance with the reception rules contained in the 2006 Directive Following the action brough by the Commission (C-297/08), on the 4

4 "However, if that situation persists and leads in particular to a significant deterioration in the environment over a protracted period without any action being taken by the competent authorities, it may be an indication that the Member States have exceeded the discretion conferred on them by that provision." See Case C-365/97, *Commission v. Italy* [1999] ECR I-7773, para. 67.

5 Case C-297/08 *European Commission v. Italian Republic* [2010] ECR I-01749 (Infringement proceeding No. 2007/2195).

6 In the letter of formal notice the EU Commission criticized ineffectiveness of measures provided by decree-law No. 61/2007 for the creation of an integrated network of collection and disposal of waste.

March 2010, that, as a result of non-compliance in the adoption for the Campania region of all those measures necessary to ensure that waste was collected or disposed without danger for public health and without damaging the environment, and specifically, for failure to create an adequate and integrated network of disposal plans, with Articles 4 and 5 of the 2006/12/EC Directives. In pronouncing the sentence, the Court also ruled that with the aim of creating an integrated and adequate network of refuse disposal, every Member State disposes off a margin of discretion in the choice of the most adequate territorial base to attain national self-sufficiency.[7]

From the reconstruction of the non-compliance procedure on waste in Campania, we can acquire some useful indications, referring to both Italy's non-compliance with European legislation and the implementation of the national legislation concerning waste. The first consideration concerns the context. What happened in Campania is part of a general picture in which Italy is consistently non-compliant with the European legislation on waste. Italian policy on this topic is still based on complex and ambiguous mechanisms both from the point of view of the legislation and from the point of view of the attribution of competences and "responsibility between the levels of government agencies or management organisms". Today, the latter are governed principally by mechanisms of a regulative type which, while prohibiting dangerous behaviours and rewarding virtuous practices, require strong regulative authorities provided with command and control capacities and able to combine technical-scientific expertise with demands of an economic-social type. However, what is missing in the case of waste is a combination of "compact and flexible" regulative strategies, well-integrated with market tools, controls, both informative as well as cognitive, environmental educational tools and awareness of alternative choices and behaviour.[8]

### *7.2.2 Water Conservation*

European legislation on water has a long history: since the 1960, there has been a frantic proliferation of directives and decisions.

---

7 It was also pointed out in this Judgment that "where a Member State has specially opted, as part of one or more of its 'waste management plans' within the meaning of Art. 7(1) of Directive 2006/12, to organise the equipping of its territory on a regional basis, it should be inferred from this that each region with a regional plan must, as a rule, ensure the treatment and disposal of its waste as close as possible to the place where it is produced". Case C-297/08, *European Commission v. Italian Republic* [2010] I-01749.

8 As documented in the message of Environment Commissioner Janez Potočnik of 29 September 2011 "after more than one year from the judgment the Italian state has not yet implemented what the Court of Justice decided". In the second letter of formal notice, the European Commission stated that "the Italian authorities have adopted various measures to improve the system of waste management in Campania compared to the situation in March 2008", but they also noted that the authorities "have not yet complied with the judgment of the Court of Justice".

In 2000, many of these provisions converged in a framework directive of the European Parliament and Council, which contains the main guidelines of the European action and the definition of its aims.[9] However, such intervention did not eliminate the validity of provisions of the multiple sector directives, which have followed in the regulation of the matter over a period of thirty years. Among these, there is one in particular whose implementation has met with strong resistance over the years, both in Italy and in other Member States: it concerns Directive 91/271/CEE which legislates the treatment of urban sewage. Italy's transposition of this discipline was difficult and delayed, leading the Commission to open numerous infringement proceedings since the nineties.

While writing, two procedures for non-compliance with the legislation regarding the treatment of sewage have been opened against Italy: 2009/2034 and 2004/2034.[10] In particular for the latter on the 5 May 2010, the European Commission resolved to defer Italy to the European Court of Justice for non-compliance of some "urban areas" to the requirements set out by the Directive 91/271/CEE.[11] Both procedures manifest the existence of serious malfunctions in the transposition phase of the European rules. There are essentially two reasons why the mechanism created in Italy to transpose the directive first with the Delegated Decree 152/1999, and then with the Delegated Decree 152/2006 failed to produce good results. Above all, although transposed, the provisions of the Directive 91/271/CEE remained on paper for a long period.[12] The second failure can be traced back to the execution phase of the legislation, above all in the definition of both the procedures and of the decisional mechanisms. In the water sector, more than in any other, there is a clear ambiguity underlying the provision: if, on one hand, all the most important decisions concerning the Environmental Code are attractive to the executive of the Ministry for the Environment and the Cabinet, such as the classification of the area and the elaboration of basin plans, on the other, such provisions award the basin authorities the management of the ambits and the decisions at the most operative level, leaving only a few marginal aspects relating to the definition of these plans to the region. From the examination of these two cases, two types of reasoned opinions can be attained. First, in many cases the *non-implementation of rules goes hand in hand with the ambiguity of the competences between State, regions and local authorities*. The best solution to solve this problem is surely that of moving from a fragmented consideration of different interests, to an integrated and harmonious management of water policies. Furthermore, it is above all when dealing

9 Directive 2000/60/EC of the European Parliament and of the Council establishing a framework for the Community action in the field of water policy.

10 In addition there are other infringement proceedings already initiated and concluded against Italy for breach of EU law in relation to a single public infrastructure. See, for example, Procedure no. 2000/5152, Case C-293/05.

11 In the "reasoned opinion" released on 19 May 2011 the Commission affirmed that the Italian Republic had in a "general and persistent" manner infringed the above mentioned Directive.

12 For a long time the Italian Government has not sent data on the monitoring of wastewater, and when it did, it was only under the pressure of an infringement procedure.

with the perspectives of the European discipline, that the classic issues of the competences between state and regions assume a different value, no longer necessarily oriented towards a conflict, but towards the *integration of responsibilities*. The objectives followed by European policy, such as the reduction of the risk of accidental pollution of the basins allocated to the collection of water and to water supplies, the regular updating of the data concerning compliance to the legislation required from private and public agencies with regard to the use, the production and discharge of polluting and dangerous substances, are occasions in which the role of the territorial authorities should emphasize coordination and harmony with a view to preventing catastrophic events. Second, from the framework of infringements in the matter of compliance with the legislation concerning sewage, a further factor emerges, which characterizes the problem of the transposition of European law: in Italy, as well as in many other Member States, a situation of non-compliance frequently arises, not because transposition is given to European directives but because of *an omitted communication to the Commission of the national measures of execution of the directive itself*; subsequently, where the implementation is executed, frequently the provisions adopted result as being unsuitable to efficiently transpose the established dictates and validly follow the environmental objectives desired by the European Legislator.

### *7.2.3 Wildlife Protection*

Within the wildlife protection framework, "hunting dispensation" is the most problematic sector.[13] Hence, the Italian legislation has often been subject to infringement proceedings. Among all, we report infringement No. 2006/2131, concerning the incorrect application of the provisions contained in the directive 79/409/CEE on the "Conservation of wild birds". This procedure regards the legislation of hunting in a large number of Italian regions. With the Judgment dated 15 July 2010 (C-573/08) the Court of Justice sanctioned Italy for inadequate compliance with the internal provisions of Directive 79/409/CEE. The aforementioned directive concerning the conservation of all the species of live birds aimed at ensuring their protection, management, regulation pertaining to their exploitation, dictates rigorous and precise indications concerning hunting quotas. Such strict and binding regimes can only and exclusively be avoided by Member States in the cases in which no other satisfactory solutions are available and for the reasons strictly indicated. In order to clearly identify the limits wherein the internal provisions can extend in defining the exemptions, the aforementioned articles state that the exemption clauses must, in any case mention all the elements aimed at demonstrating their exceptional nature. Furthermore, the directive includes the forwarding of an annual report on the application

13 The notions of "exceptional hunting" is meant to refer to the inclusion of a species not hunted in the list of huntable with a derogation to its status as a protected species.

of the exemption clause from every single state to the Commission, in order to evaluate when the latter is not compliant with European law. In Italy, Directive 79/409/CEE was interpreted in part by Law 221/2002. This law functions as "framework legislation" in so much as it defines only the general elements of the issue, leaving the region responsible for the implementation of the dispensations. This involves the presence of an ulterior provision at regional level which identifies the rules on the basis of which the dispensations to the directive can be authorized.

In the aforementioned infringement proceedings, the Commission censured four aspects of the regional legislation. First, the omitted indication of the motives that legitimize the dispensation by the regions. According to the Commission, the regional laws generically mention the aim of prevention of damage to crops without indicating the reasons for which the dispensation provisions are attributable to such an aim and therefore without explaining the connection between the need for prevention and the killing of a specific species of birds. Second, the legislation lacks scientific evidence produced by the agencies authorized by public legislation. On the basis of the framework legislation, it is the responsibility of the National Institute for Wildlife (INFS) to establish the maximum number of killings for every species in every region. This procedure is needed to implement the system that identifies the so-called "small quantity" on a national scale. The INFS act does not define the hunting limits but only the maximum number of birds that can be killed. Therefore, on the basis of this procedure, it is not correct to use the INFS decision many Italian regions as do in order to establish the dispensation quota.

Thirdly, another aspect constitutes a relevant failure in the compliance stage, and concerns the general and abstract characteristic of the provisions wherein the huntable species are identified on the basis of the dispensation, which in so far as it is an exceptional event should have a quota value. With exception to those laws that establish a dispensation valid for a singular hunting season, the Commission does not consider compliant to the 1979 directive the regional laws that contain the explicit indications of the species which can be the object of the dispensation in accordance with (as they already identify, in a general and abstract manner, and with no existing time limits) the species covered by the dispensation and in this way diverge from the intention of the directive to conceive the dispensation itself as an exceptional measure of a "provisional" nature which is adopted on the basis of a precise and prompt analysis of the requirements and of the conditions established *de facto* by the article.

It is as if to say that the dispensation organization system should discipline the methods, the procedures and the attributions to the competent authorities, but cannot identify the object of the dispensation in advance, as this is the result of the analysis of a factual situation that varies from time to time.

The fourth observation put forward by the Commission is even more decisive, relating to the fact that the listing of the species which can be hunted under dispensation in the attachment to the regional laws, could be considered compliant with the directive only when the law itself provides a true yearly revision on the basis of the effective confirmation of the requirements and conditions described in Article 9 of the directive. This precision is significantly important. The violation of the EU Law implemented by the Italian authorities derives precisely from *the non-application of a correct harmonization of internal rules*. Furthermore, it involves a "'constant violation which produces a persistent and structural' consequence in the Italian system of reception and transposition". This observation is connected to another particularly relevant aspect in the ambit of transposition of European law: all the "legislative procedure provided for in Italy for hunting dispensations" and, in particular, the part which concerns state control over regional dispensations conflicts with the legislation provided by the 1979 Directive. Article 19-bis of the 1992 Law introduced by the transposition law 221/2002, in fact, provides an articulated procedure with numerous decisional passages, which, in fact makes state control completely ineffective as it usually only arises at the moment in which the dispensations provided by regional laws have exhausted their effect.

The dispensations to regional laws, therefore, make the legitimate control foreseen by national Law ineffective, giving rise to a "semi permanent regime of the hunting of birds whose hunting is prohibited".

### *7.2.4 Air Protection*

The legislation concerning the quality of air, which is articulated in several sectors (*e.g.* the discipline on pollution produced by motor vehicles, the legislation on emissions produced by industrial plants and incinerators of urban refuse), is constantly under the vigilant eye of the European Commission.[14] The common aim is to establish legislation pertaining to quality, value limits, value guidelines and alarm levels relating to the emission of singular polluting factors in the atmosphere, in order to reduce the negative effects on the atmosphere, as well as to guarantee the alignment of the Member States in order to avoid conditions of unfair competition and market malfunctioning.

The EU has also intervened on the value limits for the dangerous particles transported in the air, identified by code PM10.[15] European law provides that Member States adopt all the necessary measures to avoid a concentration of PM10 particles in the air, which exceeds the prescribed level limits. Moreover, Member States have to complete a detailed report every

14 See Directives 70/156/EEC, 70/220/EEC, 72/306/EEC. With regard to the regulation of emissions from industrial plants and incineration, see Directives 84/360/EEC and more recently 2004/76/EC.

15 See Directives 96/62/EC, 99/30/EC and 2008/50/EC.

year with regard to the transposition state of the legislation. The Directive 2008/50/CE then extended favourable terms towards the States, which, in particular circumstances may ask for a limited extension in order to comply with the value limits of PM10.[16]

The contemporaneousness between an infringement proceeding and a request for extension is an exceptional event that is worth taking into consideration starting from the review of an infringement proceeding culminating with an appeal to the Court of Justice (Case C-68/11). During the verification of the PM10 pollution levels, the Commission found that in many parts of Italy, the limits established by the 1999 Directive[17] had been exceeded. Thus, the Commission asked for data concerning the implementation measures already adopted or provided for in order to comply with and respect the conditions for a possible extension of the period relating to the transposition to the ongoing directive (2008/50/EC).

Subsequent to a formal confirmation, the Commission warned Italy that it would be starting an infringement procedure by 20 January 2008. At this point, the Italian Ministry for the Environment implemented the activity of coordination of all the regions and supplied the data relating to the areas that gave most cause for concern, above all for the orographic and climatic conditions.

The communications delivered by the Ministry showed the progress achieved in the reduction of PM10 values in many areas, but the lack of a formal request for a derogation led the Commission to decide to send a letter of formal notice (29 January 2009) in which it protested the violation of Article 5 of Directive 1999/30/EC. In reality, a registered letter with a request for a derogation relating to Article 22 had been sent by Italy precisely in that period.[18] The Commission however, felt this statement was incomplete for two reasons: 1) an implementation plan of the "national planning document" mentioned in the derogation request had not been sent and 2) a request for a derogation was missing for some regions (Campania, Puglia and Sicilia) in which there were areas whose values exceeded the limits prescribed, but for which the relative provisions had not been implemented.

The Commission replied to Italy's request for a derogation with two decisions in September 2009 and in February 2010. The authorization was accorded in only a partially positive sense: for some areas and only up to June 2011. This answer was predictable both in the light of Italy's difficulty to come back down to below the value limits of PM10 established

16 Italy has formally asked twice to the Commission an extension for some specific areas. The Commission responded with two decisions accepting only partially requests made by the Italian State. See Decisions [2009] C-7390 and [2010] C-490.

17 Together with Italy, nine other EU countries were joined by a warning for violation of the thresholds of PM10. Source: "Rapid" programme of European Commission (IP/09/174, 29 January 2009).

18 See Communication of Commission COM(2009) 7390 (first recital).

by the 1999 directive, and the peculiar orographic conditions of the places involved, combined with the inflexibility shown by the Commission in the implementation of the legislative rules concerning air protection. Another fact of relevant importance exists however: the EU decision depended mainly on the lack of data supplied by Italy. Indeed, the data deficiency has, on one hand, demonstrated that Italy had exceeded the values, and on the other, it has not allowed the identification of the causes.[19] On 5 May 2010, the Commission sent a reasoned opinion in which it renewed the allegation of violation and ascertained the inexistence of a national package of legislative and regulative measures that would help in the difficult task of reducing not only the quantity of PM10 but also the polluting factors. Although the Ministry for the Environment was aware of the aforementioned facts, as emerges from the reply to the Commission (5 July 2010), Italy did not provide data on the adoption of a package of measures within the prescribed time. For this reason, in November 2010, the Commission deferred Italy to the ECJ.

### *7.2.5 Environmental Risk*

The question of the control of environmental risk has been the object of numerous interventions at European level, above all concerning the environmental impact assessment (EIA) and strategic environmental assessment (SEA): the first disciplined through Directive 85/337/CEE and the second through Directive 2001/42/CE. The latter, in particular, was blocked for a considerable time before being implemented in almost half of the Member States to the point that in 2005 the Commission commenced infringement proceedings towards all non-compliant countries, including Italy,[20] which then proceeded to transpose the second part of the Delegated Decree 152/2006 (Environmental Consolidated Act).

An example of the difficulty in implementing the rules concerning strategic environmental assessment (SEA) involved Italy. This case led to the opening of procedure 2009/2235. In this procedure the Commission contested the non-compliance with the obligations referred to in Articles 7, 8 and 9, paragraph 1 of the SEA directive, for not having defined appropriate regulations with regard to trans-boundary consultations in Article 32 of the Delegated Decree 152/2006, and having incorrectly transposed the regulations of Article 8 of the directive, which regulates the evaluation of environmental assessment, the results of consultation and the decision on plans and programmes submitted for evaluation into Articles 15 and 16.

19 In addition, the measures set out in the plans sent from Italy have not shown clearly how the State would satisfy European predictions at the end of the extension period.

20 The Court of Justice condemned Italy on 8 November 2007 (Case C-40/07).

Although the procedure had highlighted a problem of incorrect application, Italy was able to resolve the question through legislative means by simply modifying Articles 15 and 32 of the Environmental Consolidated Act.
With reference to Article 15, it was clarified that if there exists a contrast between a SEA plan or program, or reasoned opinion, the first should be modified to render it compatible with the second, while with reference to Article 32 the legislative modification prescribed the obligation of the participation of the states in the identification procedure of plans, programmes and projects which could have a significant impact on the environment of another state. Furthermore, Article 32-bis was added, which provided for the obligation of communication in those cases where a plant can have negative or significant effects on the environment of another state. This issue clearly shows how the observations made in proper time by the Commission are, sometimes, taken into consideration by the competent state authorities. In this specific case however, although it is only the result of a legislative provision and therefore still to be verified in the administrative practice, the modifications to the Environment Consolidated Act provided for in the Delegated Decree 128/2010 are evidently the effect of the transposition of the concerns originating from European Institutions. This is evident in the fact that not only the singular provisions on which the Commission concentrated are being examined by the Italian Government, but also are further provisions that form the overall SEA framework. Therefore, it could be said that the regulatory intervention is not merely a "formal" fulfilment, implemented to include an erroneously unforeseen regulation into the legal system, but it shows how the infringement procedure operates as a motivational tool for improvement of the national legal system.

## 7.3 ANALYSIS

The study of some of the procedures concerning Italy highlights how the correct transposition of European obligations is negatively influenced by malpractice, procedural or structural defects. There is a close correlation between the tendency of national and regional legislators to an insufficient analysis of the European demand for harmonization and incomplete or deformed answers to the requests. In addition to the malfunctions at legislative level there are also the low standards of consciousness of the transposition mechanisms and, often the structural incapacity of local and national administrations. Furthermore, Italy presents a system of harmonization policies and application procedures that has proven to be, at least up to now, inadequate. Finally, as a result of the careful examination of the cases, the aforementioned problems often overlap to create a complex system of malfunction.

### 7.3.1 The Causes of Environmental Non-Compliance

*What are the causes of environmental non-compliance?*[21] Two theories are usually used in order to respond to this question. First, the causes of implementation difficulty can be traced back to the *heterogeneity of the area within which the implementation is to be performed*: the policies from which European directives originate do not take into account the important difference between the administrative traditions of the different countries. Therefore, it could be said that frequently European political choices and legislation are characterized by the "implementation germ".

The second theory, however, highlights that the non-compliance is linked to the institutional characteristics of the European political system capable of creating for itself a radical pathology of non-implementation. For a long time, the European institutional architecture favoured a clear separation between the moment of policy formation and the moment of transposition. This has often induced the European institution to formulate ambitious provisions, which in practice transfer an enormous implementation burden onto the Member State. The reason for such difficulty can be explained through the most elementary categories of law: European law is a law of an external legal system which must first be transposed according to internal constitutional rules and then implemented at an administrative level.

The two problems mentioned characterize all political sectors, in which, on one hand, the *global dimension of problems coexists with the local destination of their implementation* and on the other, the *unitary origin of policies* (Brussels and European institutions) *coexists with the heterogeneity of the final executors* (Member States, territorial administrations and other interested public and private authorities).

Moreover, other profiles of criticism characterize the specific political sector under examination: the environment is, in fact, at the same time 1) a convergence point of a plurality of conflicting interests; 2) a privileged ambit for regulations of technical nature; 3) a matter on which several decisional bodies share competence; 4) a field in which continuous emergencies are involved.

These criticisms obviously generate a series of issues that cannot be easily resolved. We shall try to analyze the four highlighted aspects.

With regard to the first profile, the EU national and local level have attempted to find a solution to the issues relating to the intersectoral of the environment through the creation of specialized administrative authorities, the so-called Environmental Agencies.[22] These agencies operate to assess the feasibility and the impact of environmental regulations on the interests affected. The Agency system should prevent the "conflicts"

21 See the Report of 2008: EUROPEAN COMMISSION, *Handbook on the Implementation of EC Environmental Legislation*, 2008 (<http://ec.europa.eu/environment/enlarg/handbook/handbook.htm>).

22 Such as EPA, EIONET, IMPEL, etc.

between the various stakeholders. However, even when they are diffused, the agencies are unable to foresee and therefore prevent the impediments of the territorial, social, economic productive nature which can arise during the long implementation procedure. The obstacles also derive from the convergence of a plurality of contrasting interests in the environmental matters that involve every level of the implementation process. During the formation phase of the European acts for instance, Parliament is seen as a representative authority of the widespread interest in environmental protection while the Council tends to operate as holder of the economical interest of the industrialist lobbies.

With regard to the second profile, environmental provisions are intrinsically a technical discipline. Article 191(3) TFEU includes, among the prerequisites relating to regulations in environmental matters, the acquisition and the consciousness of scientific data and technicians available.[23] The same fundamental principles of prevention and precaution require the acquisition and processing of technical data. Therefore, environmental matters, for their particular nature, require a clear repartition of competences with regard to the political choices, underlining technical regulations, an efficient network of experts and structures as well as a concrete possibility to find active and capable technicians within the assigned administrations.

With regard to the third profile, the distribution of environmental competences is not simple, due to the intention to give power to the local communities that express the needs of those who live in close contact with the surrounding environment, and the need to keep the major part of decisional power on higher levels, where wide scale phenomena are better regulated. Each of these incentives evidently produces a series of problems. It is sufficient to remember that in the Italian constitution, compared with an at least apparent inflexibility of the repartition of competences there is no correspondence with an equally defined distribution of competencies among the authorities involved.[24]

Finally, the fourth profile. Compliance is undoubtedly an obligation of the national institutions for which they are responsible in virtue of their affiliation in processes of European transposition. However, the national dimension and its authorities delegated to compliance must inevitably confront the restrictions deriving from the local circumstances of the final destination for the concrete effects of European regulations (*e.g.* the case of "waste disposal emergency" in the Campania region).

### *7.3.2 The Main Impediments to Compliance*

The achievement of an improved efficiency in European transposition that involves all levels of governments from European to national on the basis of the principle of

23 Italian Constitutional Court, judgment No. 31/2001 and No. 282/2002.
24 See Italian Constitutional Court, judgment No. 407/2002, No. 367 and 378/2007 and No. 225/2009.

harmonization, has to deal with two problems: the first concerns the definition of the time for the transposition of the regulations; the second concerns the sharing of responsibilities among the levels of governments charged with the execution of regulations.

The first obstacle to be taken into account is the following: the environment is a notoriously hyper-regulated sector with norms of elevated technical – scientific content and difficult to manage from a socio-political point of view. In the environmental field it is common practice not to decide or to let others decide. Acknowledging such a limit, it is evident that the discipline of certain phenomena is not necessarily opportune but also essential. The reduction of pollution or waste processing are issues that cannot be delayed, but on the contrary should be decided in the shortest possible time. Deciding requires both industry knowledge on which to intervene and the assessment of the effect of the decision itself. The reconstruction of the complexity of regulations and the definition of the framework of actions that derive from a centralized decision represent the first action that can resolve any implementation failure.

In political terms, this involves the creation of a cognitive apparatus which allows the identification of the framework of the decisions taken, and those to be taken. One example can help to define this statement: examining of infringement proceedings, discovered that the Department for European Policies, through an Infringements Taskforce, the so-called "Struttura di Missione", organizes and shares periodical meetings between the Commission delegations and the administrations involved in an infringement proceeding. These so-called "package meetings" are intended to identify the non-compliances and to set a work schedule to respond to the requirements of the Commission contained, for instance, in the letter of formal notice. This is the way for the department to acquire useful information to start a dialogue with the Commission aimed at reaching a solution for the infringement procedure. In our view, such actions, performed only in the presence of a failure to comply, could be usefully activated prior to the moment of transposition of the European law.

The second obstacle in the field of environmental law is a sheer mismatch between responsibility and competence. The public sector often struggles with execution of EU directives and therefore tends to manage every matter as urgent (*logica dell'emergenza*) instead of being able to have a programmatic approach. Returning to the cases examined, it is evident in each one of them that at European level the strategies of the administrative transposition are conceived in different ways: depending on the results to be achieved. On a national level however, there is not only the need to integrate the various actions according to pre-established objectives but there is also the need for a different course of action at an administrative level based on the logics of harmonization and in accordance with the development of four distinct stages: consciousness, planning, verification and assessment.

### 7.3.3 *Harmonization Perspective*

The problems of implementation require us to focus on the transposition process undertaken in order to adjust national legislation to European laws. The directive is also a tool that requires for national law an alignment process in view of the pursuit of common objectives while allowing for local specificity. Such actions, implemented on a supernational level, are aimed at the integration of the national legal regulations and of the legal alignment of Member States: in international language, it goes by the name of "harmonization". The harmonization requires the existence of several regulations to coordinate and the need to eliminate any impediment of a technical, administrative or provisional nature involving the transposition of EU legislation within the singular Member States.
On an entirely operative level, the harmonization is made through directives. They set up the most adequate vehicle to perform harmonizaton. In broad terms, the harmonization process implies three different actions. The first consists in the formation of the harmonizing legislation; the second is that of transposition of the *supra*-national dispositions within the national legislative system; the third is the execution of national law implemented on the basis of the indications originating from the super-national law. Harmonization through the directives leaves the national authorities interventional discretion, and therefore gives them a choice concerning the forms and tools which are most suitable for the transposition as well as authorities from whom compliance is required on the basis of internal repartition of competences. A positive confirmation of this operative system is to be found in the TFEU, and in particular in its title 1, part 1 which deals with "categories and sectors of EU competence". On the basis of Article 4(2), the environmental issues belong to the category of parallel competences on which the State, while allowing for European legislation, can "make laws and adopt legally-binding acts". This independence to make laws is expressed in different ways depending on whether the EU enacts common directives from which the state cannot distance itself, or it limits itself to imposing a minimum level of legislation. In the first case, the discretional margin conceded to the States tends to almost disappear; in the second, the States can provide a higher level of protection with their independent policy. The harmonization tool is operative in both cases limiting or extending the margin of discretion left to the state depending on the scope it intends to pursue.
With regard to environmental matters, European institutions frequently use both one and the other harmonization techniques. The first is defined as total harmonization, and exists when a directive provides total uniformity without legal derogations of the Member States. The second harmonization method is, however, called minimal or partial.
This second variation can be defined as a procedure conseding to Member States the competence to adopt stricter environmental standards than those set out in the European legislation. This type of harmonization is often used in sectors in which differences among

national standards have nothing to do with the national market (*e.g.* quality of water, of air, waste, radiation protection or other polluting agents). The regulations which have this type of harmonization are easy to recognize.[25] They are characterized by the margin they leave Member States in providing for more or less strict measures, except in the hypothesis that they create impediments to trade and commerce when the values set out in the directive are exceeded.

### *7.3.4 The Emergence of a Different Reconstruction Hypothesis*

The argumentation aimed at identifying the reasons underlying the lack of implementation of European Legislation made it possible to highlight that the degree of Europeanization reached by the Italian Environmental Law is not only the result of the mechanisms we might call "positive" relating to the alignment. This process includes also the moment of verification of correct compliance, and therefore the infringement proceeding for non-compliance; for this reason the latter aspect can be referred to as a "positive" figure of the defects of harmonization.

Data used in this chapter make clear that the Italian failure in the transposition of European environmental legislation is still considerable. The difficulty encountered in the compliance mechanism concerning European standards derives mainly from the lack of institutional and procedural changes capable of intercepting the objectives set out in the directives.

In two thirds of the procedures, regions and local authorities are responsible for the failure and almost all the failures relate to violations due to poor administrative enforcement of state legislation transposing the European legislation.[26]

Although the deficit emerges in the form of a lack of adaptation by regional and local governments as institutions to the objectives of the standards of the European Community regulations, the substance and the root of the failure seem to lie elsewhere. Regional and local governments find often difficulties in applying the national legislation. On the basis of our study even problems in the administrative execution have yet an origin in the implementation stage. Ambiguous transposition of directives generates a distortion in the regulation "outcome". This is evident whenever we find a non-compliance in the use of all the possibilities inherent to the activity of discretionary implementation of the

25 These directives contain the following wording "Member States may, at any time, fix values more stringent than those laid down in this Directive". See, for example, Art. 5 of Directive 85/203/ECC on air quality standards for nitrogen dioxide.

26 If we look at the judgments within a infringement proceedings, we note that the majority ascertains the cause of failures exclusively or primarily relate to the implementation of environmental standards at the local level.

environmental directives.[27] The simplest example to demonstrate the consistency of this distortion is the so-called "automatic transposition", that is the approval by Parliament or regional Councils of regulations that merely repeat the provisions contained in the directives. This mechanism, as can be easily imagined, on one hand allows the legislator to rapidly fulfil obligations without much effort, but on the other hand excludes the insertion into the national or regional legislation of the tools and mechanisms which can transpose the objectives of the directives to the conditions and specific circumstances in which the fulfilment occurs. In those cases examined, instead of achieving the harmonization of its own laws to the objectives of the directives, the state tends to act as a passive receptor of the legislation. In this way, the potential inherent to the techniques of harmonization adopted at European level is lost, with the effect of failing the transposition target of the existing rules with the new rules for the implementation of directives. In these cases, the transposition phase of the European rules is detached from the moment of coordination between the authorities which are responsible for administrative implementation. In our opinion, what is described in the aforementioned cases produces a particular form of misuse in the exercise of discretion conceded by European law, in which national or regional laws appear to conform to EU legislation while in practice there is a lack of tools for compliance. The same bodies responsible for the implementation do not create the conditions (*i.e.* the dialogue) for compliance.[28] The hypothesis we intend to pursue takes into consideration the entity of the actions taken within the state as a phenomenon that requires, above all, a correct use of sources in the light of the principle of European harmonization. The case studies demonstrate the need to extend the harmonizing perspective from the EU Member States' relationship to that of the relations among local governments (regions, provinces, municipalities, etc.). The process of continuous implementation of European law needs to adapt and to define the architecture of an implementation system that is oriented to a logic of harmonization at all levels, both in terms of relations between institutions and in terms of connections between different sources of law.

## 7.4 CONCLUSIONS

As set out in the introduction, the purpose of our study aimed to reveal how the implementation deficit of European law locally, is not merely limited to political oppositions, but it is also due to technical and legal matters. We tried to emphasize how the main tool to solve this failure within the implementation process is the correct use of the principles of harmonization from both an institutional and functional point of view. The process to

27 See, for example, Cases C-82/06 and C-68/11.

28 See, for example, the judgment on the assessment of the effects of certain plans and programmes on the environment (Case C-40/07).

transpose the implementation of European law is connected to some choices regarding the correct use of European sources, either for the objectives they describe or for the required organization. The strategies designed at European level require decisions involving all the implementation agents from the onset. Political actions are not parallel to coordination objectives and to some extend tend to develop a system, where despite appearing *prima facie* in complying with directives from Brussels, it will continue to produce significant implementation failures.

# 8 Infringement Proceedings Between Law and Practice

*Angela Cossiri*

## 8.1 Scope of the Study[1]

The chapter analyzes the administrative management of the non-compliances for which notification has been given by the European Commission from the time of the informal notification following a private or official charge (the so-called pre-infringement stage). In cases where this first assessment does not lead to the case being closed, a letter of formal notice of the opening of infringement proceedings will be given. The conclusion of these proceedings normally takes place after the Italian state fulfils its obligations and only on one recent occasion it led to the application of financial penalties as provided by the treaties.[2] The analysis is carried out with particular reference to environmental matters as limited in the legal basis of the Treaty on the Functioning of the European Union (EU).
The study of practices will help to shed light on important aspects of the relationships between the systems relevant to the systematic profile and will help to identify the critical issues emerging and on which reasons and solutions need to be considered.
Some particularly significant cases have also been selected in order to identify the causes of the non-compliances and to examine what tools may be useful in improving the fulfilment of the obligations of European law by the national system.

## 8.2 Administration of Non-Compliance by the State Between Law and Practice

The Department for European Policies, established with Law 183/1987, is the structure on which the President of the Council of Ministers relies for the management of relations between the Italian Government and the EU institutions. In particular, it is responsible

1 This study is mainly the result of a survey of empirical investigation files relating to objections raised by the Commission to the Italian State, held at the Department for European Policies at the Presidency of the Council of Ministers. The author would like to thank the Head of Department, Prof. Robert Adam, for allowing the research work at the Office, and Dr. Caterina Gestri for their valuable assistance. The task was closed on 15 March 2012 and all dates referred to, should be in reference to this date.

2 See Case C-496/09 [2011] ECR, delivered in the case concerning the non-recovery of state aid with regard to contracts of training and work.

for coordination between internal administrations who are responsible at the time of the shaping of the EU legislation and when it is introduced into Italian law. Among the many tasks that were carried out for this study, the activity of management of non-compliance allegations is highlighted, directed on the one hand at preventing the occurrence of offences of this nature and on the other aimed at coordinating and supporting actions aimed at finding solutions to the objections raised by the Commission, functions that are specifically dealt with by a Mission Structure set up in 2006.

The central role of this structure in the management of complaints of non-compliance is externally formalized in its role as a "national contact point" for EU-Pilot, the administrative tool of the preliminary stage of the opening of an infringement proceeding adopted by the Commission from 2008 and used by fifteen Member States on a voluntary basis.

The mission structure comes into force in the stage between national law and EU law and is activated from the moment the non-compliance is formulated with the aim of preventing the opening of an infringement proceedings. Once the Commission has cited specific complaints and requests for information, the structure is responsible for providing assistance and support to public administrations involved in the specific non-compliance that follows. Moreover, if more than one subject or territorial administrative level is involved, it ensures coordination of their activities in order to define the position to be presented to the Commission, mainly through the convening of meetings and conferences in Italy and Brussels.

This structure does not have decision-making powers. Therefore the adoption of the obligations remains a question of the government's willingness according to the division of powers ordinarily provided by law among the various levels of government. However, in practice, the structure is largely responsible for coordination in response to the concrete needs that arise during the infringement proceedings and actively assists the bodies involved.

Even if official recipient of all formal notifications from the EU is the Ministry of Foreign Affairs, the Mission Structure directly handles the relations with the European institutions so as to be the only interlocutor responsible for the management of non-compliance and therefore in a position to promote a collaborative dialogue with the supra-national level.

The activities that follow the notification clearly require adequate knowledge of the EU legal system, its internal organization and its negotiating methods and therefore require specialist skills that in most cases are not available within the administration, especially when local levels of government are involved.

The structure does not have any coordination responsibility regarding any judicial consequences of the pre-litigation stage if there is a negative outcome. This is the responsibility of the Ministry of Foreign Affairs, called upon to define the defence strategy, and of the Attorney General's office which is involved from the moment the case is opened in the previous stage.

In terms of the amount of litigation handled and resolved administratively through the Mission Structure in the pre-infringement and pre-litigation stages, roughly half of the EU-Pilot cases are closed and less than 20% of open infringement proceedings against the Italian state continue up to the judicial phase of proceedings before the Court of Justice. The Mission Structure also acts as the liaison office between the Government and the bodies of political control and accounting. The structure provides information to the European Parliament and the Court of Auditors on the progress of the pre-litigation (*i.e.* only from the moment that formal infringement proceedings are launched) and litigation, and supports the Ministry of Economy and Finance in preparing a report on the financial implications of the infringements.

## 8.3 Working Methods in the Administrative Stage

The operational instrument for the administration management of the "litigation" includes the so-called "package meetings". The meetings, chaired by the Department for European Policies, carry out a joint examination together with the Commission and national administrations involved in a "package" of open cases or infringements relating to the same matter. This practice is adopted by the Commission and regards all the Member States, although documentation is not easy to come by.

As often happens in the EU, good results are obtained through informal dialogue during negotiations. The ability to provide direct and immediate clarifications and all relevant information is crucial in these processes. So, this type of meeting as opposed to the traditional instruments and formal management reports makes it easier to find common solutions and promotes a positive outcome of many proceedings that are already open or are in the complaint stage.

The case management is also carried out by organizing and coordinating further meetings in Brussels between the central or local government authorities and the Commission services. These meetings provide an opportunity for clarification or for specific commitments to be agreed upon, where the discussion of individual infringement proceedings is particularly difficult.

From 2008, in case different levels of government are involved in the non-compliance, the management practices of the state are formalized in a coordinated agreement between the Government, the regions, the autonomous provinces, municipalities and mountain communities "on the implementation of the obligations arising from Italy's membership to the EU and on the guarantees of information by the Government". With this agreement, the bodies represented, while reiterating their undertaking to fully cooperate to ensure timely adjustment of their respective obligations under Union law, jointly commit to adopt all necessary measures. In particular, the government guarantees to local governments prompt and complete information relating to the infringement proceedings or relating to the requests for formal information on the part of the Commission during the whole process; for their part, the regions and provinces undertake to send the necessary reports to the Government within the set time limit. The management of the exchange of information and the convening of meetings between the administrations concerned is always coordinated through the Department for European Policies.

The centralized organizational model chosen and the informal methods of work adopted have shown to produce good performance results in the management of complaints: compared to the negative "peak" of 275 open cases against the Italian State as of June 2006, there was in fact a constant reduction in the total volume of open files (for example, in 2010, 93 old infringement proceedings were closed, compared with the opening of 53 new proceedings) so that by the end of 2011 there was an overall reduction of more than 50%.[3]

As will be seen, however, this positive trend in terms of quantity corresponds to an increase in the number of cases which reached an advanced stage of the infringement proceedings and therefore exposed Italy to the imminent risk of financial penalties, a clear sign that in cases (not particularly frequent) where there are serious problems of adjustment by the state to EU law, the efficient administration of the practice is not itself sufficient enough to produce good results.

## 8.4 The Pre-Infringement Stage

From an examination of the practices that characterize the application of the infringement proceedings, it is clear that the objective pursued by the Commission is never merely or primarily repressive. In all its various stages, the ultimate goal of the infringement proceedings is to obtain state compliance, together with the process of internal adjustment and possibly convincing decision makers to adopt measures that could be very expensive or politically "inconvenient". From this point of view therefore, the infringement proceeding acts as an instrument for the Commission to manage the implementation of EU law within national law in the cases that prove to be more problematic.

It would seem that the Commission is fully aware of the fact that the financial penalties represent a forceful and effective weapon of pressure and threat which however, is destined to lose its deterrent function when they are actually imposed or when the proceedings reach the stage whereby it is clear that fines will be enforced.

As is well known, the Commission is responsible for starting the proceedings and by exercising their discretionary powers, they may act *ex officio* or on the basis of a report received from external parties. In practice, cases of referral presented directly by one

3 See Department of European Policies, *La partecipazione dell'Italia all'Ue, Relazione consuntiva 2010, ex art. 1, Legge* 11/2005, available on the Department's website: <www.politichecomunitarie.it>.

Member State with reference to another pursuant to Article 259 TFEU, are very rare and, apart from a few exceptional cases only occurred a number of years ago: it seems this is also because the countries that have special interests to defend should not have any difficulty in going through unofficial channels via intermediation of private individuals, and in that way activate the Commission.

In addition to carrying out studies and surveys (*e.g.* in the assessment of the impact of adopted legislation or in the case of the so-called environmental inspections[4]), the Commission receives reports and news on a daily basis from external bodies that could be relevant to non-compliance issues: complaints and reports from citizens, bodies and private organizations; questions put by members of the European Parliament; citizens' petitions to the European Parliament pursuant to Article 227 TFEU (this is how the case was initiated on the cement on the dunes of Is Arenas in Sardinia, "Site of Community Importance" to protect nature within the meaning of the "Habitat" Directive[5]); reports submitted by the Member States who are obliged by EU legislation in force to provide periodic reports.

In practice, the majority of complaints are presented by individuals (53% of cases[6]), especially in the area of tenders (which have natural opponents) and in environmental protection matters for which local communities and organizations responsible for the protection are particularly aware.

It is worth remembering that anybody can submit a complaint covered in the Commission Communication COM(2002) 0141 without the need to demonstrate an interest in the complaint and without the need for any type of filter in accordance with a model that favours a large widespread control on the effectiveness of the law. Since 2009, the General Secretariat of the Commission has set up a filing system of complaints, and subsequent investigations which are entered in a central register known as CHAP, and from there begin their natural path.

Increasingly, the complaints are initiated following parliamentary questions, a tool used in a strategic way by members of the European Parliament to protect interests that are typically associated with the assembly. In particular, it is not uncommon that the MEPs belonging to pro-environment groups such as the Greens, make use of this tool and, more generally, of the powers that derive from belonging to a supranational institution to oppose the work of their national governments.

When a complaint is launched *ex officio*, in approximately 35% of cases,[7] it is however sometimes connected to events related to extreme media coverage and to which the Commission is obliged to intervene: an example of this is an open case regarding the

4 See Recommendation 2001/331/EC.

5 See <www.europarl.europa.eu/meetdocs/2004_2009/documents/cm/557/557184/557184it.pdf> (Case C-491/08 [2010] ECR).

6 See *28th Annual Report of the Commission on monitoring the application of Community law* (2010), 29 September 2011, COM(2011) 588 final, p. 3.

7 See *28th Annual Report of the Commission*, p. 3.

inadequacy of the waste management plant in the region of Campania, which began in 2007 following the uproar raised by the Italian and international press relating to the waste management emergency in the city of Naples.[8]

In addition to the time management during the infringement proceedings, there is a margin of unpredictability in the discretional powers exercised by the Commission regarding the decision to launch a case *ex officio*. In fact, in all other cases in which the Commission receives an external complaint, once it has been registered in the EU-Pilot database, the correspondence between the competent DG and the Member State follows a precise process, even in terms of the deadline, culminating in closure in only two situations: a) if the Commission is convinced that there is no failure to fulfil obligations on the part of the state following evidence provided by the state, b) if the state that has failed to fulfil obligations, adopts measures to comply with EU law, for example by modifying legislation. The proceduralization of power is the Commission's way of exercising its discretion and this should lead to the objective that is being pursued as a priority by the supra-national level to be reached, ie. making sure that obligations are actually fulfilled.[9]

The act that triggers the preliminary phase, comes from the Directorate General of the Commission responsible for the subject matter, who through the permanent Representation sends the Member State a letter containing the complaint: in formal terms, it is not the Commission who initiates the proceedings but a collegial body. This first act does not constitute the start of infringement proceedings since complaints are often unfounded and the Commission quickly becomes aware of this. Since 2008, the management of this preliminary phase has taken place via the EU-Pilot system, a project which Italy voluntarily adhered to right from the outset and which is replacing the traditional notifications and considering its good performance in terms of facilitating a positive solution, is destined to become the ordinary instrument in the management of all cases.[10]

As for Italy, from 22 April 2008 to 31 December 2010, 246 cases were processed through the EU-Pilot system, 122 of which were dismissed.[11] Therefore approximately only 50% of the requests for information for alleged non-compliances received from the Commission actually led to the formal opening of infringement proceedings and therefore to the pre-infringement stage.

The preliminary phase is characterized by the confidentiality of the activities carried out and of all the documents – made up essentially of correspondence and reports of the meetings. This practice is justified due to the need not to compromise negotiating in the best interest of the state when a case is successfully closed.

8 See ECR, ruling 4 March 2010, C-297/08.

9 The Commission proceeds with a suitable filter of complaints (now included in CHAP, before converging with EU-Pilot) which appear *prima facie* to be manifestly unfounded.

10 See the European Commission's Report of the EU-Pilot project management, 3 March 2010.

11 See *La partecipazione dell'Italia all'UE, Relazione consuntiva 2010*, p. 80.

However, the lack of transparency, as well as giving rise to an area exempt from controls, limits the knowledge of the external complaints and defences. An important effect – among others – is to make it impossible at this stage to systematically verify the fulfilment of the other Member States regarding the European legislation. Thus, it is very difficult to make a comparative analysis of the pre-infringement stage although it is occasionally possible to find information and in some cases to verify the existence of common problems which may depend on EU legislation, from defects in regulatory quality or editorial criticisms.

This preliminary phase may end with the case being closed or, alternatively, in the event that the observations provided by the state do not appear to be effective, the Commission offices notifies that the proceedings will be moving forward and proposes a formal opening of the infringement proceedings to the Board of Commissioners. In this case, the state discovers the reasons for the negative evaluation of the replies sent through informal contacts with the Commission or through the EU-Pilot communication system. For cases which are not closed during the informal preliminary stage described so far, there then follows the formal opening of infringement proceedings approved by the Commission.

The case of non-implementation, which according to the numbers of infringements of EU law would seem to be residual compared to other types of non-compliance (22% of cases[12]), is, with the Lisbon Treaty formally distinct from infringements of EU law (due to an incorrect transposition or failure to implement the European standards) and has an accelerated fast track which has proven to be very effective: the EU-Pilot phase does not take place and the Commission automatically sends letters of formal notice every two months including all expired directives for which the electronic notification of transposition has not been given. Therefore it is the failure to communicate the transposition or the internal act which already complies with the directive to be transposed which automatically determines the complaint according to a model that produces a kind of reversal of the burden of proof.

As a result, the referral takes place within a short time period (on average 7/8 months after the expiry of the Directive) and the ruling within 18 months following except in cases where a significant number of Member States have not promptly implemented the Directive, a situation that in practice slows down the procedure.

Under the new Article 260(3) TFEU, the Commission may ask the Court to order the Member State to pay the financial penalty following the first ruling. To cope with the consequences of this innovation that allows for the anticipation of fines following failure to fulfil obligations, the Union Law 2012, approved by the Council of Ministers in 2011, Article 1, in order to accelerate the transposition, states that the term for the exercise of the legislative mandate no longer coincides, as stated in previous EU laws, with the expiration of the period provided in each directive for its transposition, but is brought

12 See 28th Commission Report, p. 3.

forward by two months. In this way, a more rapid adaptation of Italian legislation to EU laws should be ensured, preventing infringement proceedings for failure to communicate from being launched, a danger that was not always possible to avert with the alignment of the deadlines of the legislative decrees with the deadline for transposition of the individual directives.

## 8.5 Infringement Proceedings Against the Italian State

At the end of the last monthly meeting of the Commission which was considered,[13] there were 132,95 infringement proceedings relating to infringements of EU law currently open against the Italian state (due to transposition which the Commission considered incorrect or due to the non-application of EU law); 37 were related to the failure to transpose directives.[14]

With this large number of open infringements, Italy – despite having lost its "black shirt" in 2011 – is, along with Belgium and Greece, one of the top three countries in Europe in terms of non-compliance with EU law.

This number does not really show the full extent of the phenomenon. It should be noted in fact that, in addition to questions regarding a particular event, the Commission may, following only one infringement proceeding, challenge a number of different situations of non-compliance upon which the state is called to remedy. For example, the procedure recently opened for violation of Article 14 of Directive 1999/31/EC, which requires Member States to take measures to ensure compliance with EU law of the landfill of waste existing at the time of its entry into force, on penalty of closure (recorded as 2011_2215), covers at least 102 dumps of which three refer to hazardous waste, non-compliant with EU law and located across the whole country.

The number of infringements provided reflect a relationship between the different types of infringements more or less constant over time, a phenomenon which was temporarily negative in 2010 saw an increase of the proceedings for non-transposition of directives, against the trend of a fall in infringements proceedings of EU law. This phenomenon should be attributed to the severe delay by Parliament in approving the 2010 Union law due to contingent political reasons.[15] This is a case which could theoretically be repeated

13 This refers to the meeting of 28 February 2012.

14 The figures emerge from the investigation of the EUR-Infra database, assembled and edited by the Department of European Affairs, which collects all the infringement proceedings opened against the Italian State and permits searches according to various parameters of interest, giving a comprehensive overview of the situation. This database is primarily a tool for the authorities involved in the procedures that have access to the reserved section permitting the scanning of case documents in digital form.

15 The Chamber of Deputies with a resolution of 29 June 2011 unexpectedly rejected Article 1 of the Community Bill 2010, thus blocking the approval process. The government therefore reformulated the bill, limiting the approval to the provisions that cannot be postponed.

and which is considerably risky for the responsibility of the state, especially after the amendments made by the Treaty of Lisbon regarding the lack of internal sanctions for legislative omission.

However, confirming the fact that the problems of legislative implementation do not depend on the Union law, which has proven to be an effective instrument (taking account of the number of directives to be implemented, an average of 50 per year), it should be noted that the transposition of directives whose implementation must be carried out by regulation, directly from the Government exercising jurisdiction to adopt (or amend) ministerial decrees, especially in the areas of health materials and transport, has proven to be unexpectedly problematic.

There are no cases of infringements for failure to transpose on the part of the regions, probably due to the practice of the use of compliant state regulations. However, a quarter of the total number of cases pending for violations of European law, down from 43 cases in 2008, can be attributed to the regions.

If we move on to examine which stages the open infringement proceedings have reached, we can see that more than half of the cases are in the initial stages and as far as they are concerned, the only action has been that of the formal notification from the Commission. As you would expect, the number of cases gradually decrease as the proceedings reach more advanced stages. One slightly worrying factor does however emerge: more than a quarter of the infringement proceedings pending against Italy (28 cases out of 132) have reached a particularly serious stage, or rather they have reached the stage whereby the state has been referred to the Court of Justice or even to the point that an unfavourable ruling is needed. In the short term, these are the cases that are most at risk from heavy financial penalties, therefore joint efforts should be made by all the administrations concerned to fulfil the obligations as soon as possible.

## 8.6 Italian Infringements in the Environmental Sector

The environment is by far the most problematic among all sectors (there are 33 proceedings pending), followed by taxation and customs (14), Labour and Social Affairs (12), transport (11).

We cannot automatically assume from this data that Italy has structural problems in the fulfilment of EU laws in this regard. There are numerous factors that contribute to such high numbers. First of all, the environment is an area with an enormous amount of European legislation, which affects a high proportion of national legislation, estimated at around 80%. It is known to be one of the most problematic areas even at an early stage of the adoption of legislation. It is the area in which States have most difficulty in obtaining a shared consensus, in which confrontation between the European co-legislators, the Parliament and the Council is intensified and there is the physiological difficulty of creating an effective synthesis of opposed interests especially with reference to the problem of the allocation of the costs of environmental protection. It is also an area in which the legislation reaches ambitious levels regarding environmental protection, under the pressure of the European Parliament, the strongest institution in terms of supra-national negotiation. Last but not least, it is precisely in this area that a high level of public and political interest is focused together with an attentive widespread control and the concentration of most of the complaints and complaints from associations, committees, organizations, etc. which are particularly active in Italy.[16] Finally, there are other areas in which the Commission has launched across the board investigations, monitoring the implementation of a specific directive.

The peculiarity of the "environmental" sector also emerges from the comparative analysis of the data: more than a fifth of all infringements are related precisely to European environmental legislation.[17]

Returning to the Italian State, only three cases in this sector have been opened following the failure to transpose and refer to modifications of previous directives. The non-compliances for failure to transpose can generally be resolved within a short period of time with the communication of the internal implementation which is often still being drafted. The fact that there are few cases of non-transposition is significant: it would seem that with regard to environmental protection, unlike other sectors, there is no particular resistance to the decisions on the transposition of EU law by the legislative powers. Hence we can assume that the problems that arise are confined to a later stage.

Faced with a limited number of failed transpositions, there are fourteen cases of incorrect transposition into national law of the directives or of non-compliance of national legislation and sixteen cases of non-implementation of the directives. In order to understand the causes of the failures, we must distinguish between "non-implementation" and "infringement of EU law". These two categories, as mentioned before, are formally distinguished with the Treaty of Lisbon as the first subject of accelerated infringement proceedings. It is also important to look within the types of infringements of European law at the distinction between "incorrect transposition" (*i.e.* non-conformity of national legislation with that of the EU, a critical issue that is rooted precisely in the legislative function or, in some cases, regulatory function) and the "non-application of EU law". The latter category, however, should not automatically be traced back to an infringement of an administrative nature, whose ultimate cause is a dysfunction at the time the law is applied, in other words

16 See 28th Annual Report of the Commission on monitoring the application of Community law (2010) of 29 September 2011, COM(2011) 588 final. The environmental sector is one in which the highest number of Petitions to the European Parliament was presented (120), p. 5; see also COM(2008) 773 def., 8 November 2008, p. 10: approximately 10% of all parliamentary questions to the Commission were regarding the environment.

17 See 28th Annual Report, p. 4.

an error in the exercise of administrative function. In fact, the making of laws following a correct transposition of EU law or even regarding different sectors may well frustrate the effectiveness of a law that has been transposed and adopted correctly. From this point of view, it is inadequate and the "Community" impact assessment carried out in Parliament and in regional councils in the context of the quality of legislation should be made more efficient.

The cases that have been notified as being in breach of Directive 1991/271/CE regarding the treatment of urban waste water are a good example of what has been reported. This also seems to have been caused by a senseless policy of legislative support for issuing retrospective planning permission that led to the unplanned and uncontrolled growth of urban areas with the subsequent lack of wastewater treatment and disposal plants. There is also an additional factor: the difficulty for the regional administrations to adapt the plants to the requirements in the Directive due to a lack of available financial resources.

As for the internal allocation of responsibilities between the administrations involved in the infringements, slightly less than half of the proceedings relating to the environment are the sole responsibility of regional and local authorities, while another large number of proceedings can be considered the responsibility of both the state and the regions as a result of the internal rules on the division of legislative powers or simply because the Ministry plays a leading role coordinating the various areas involved.

It should also be noted that in this area, a number of infringements are widespread across most or all of the national territory and affect many regions and local authorities. The negative record of the infringements in the environmental sector is added to by the local governments, since violations of this kind are associated with the management of the territory.

## 8.7 Analysis Cases and Causes of Non-Compliance

In this section, we have selected some of the open files that are considered particularly significant in order to provide some reconstructive hypothesis as to the causes of Italian environmental non-compliance.

### 8.7.1 *Waste Management*

The most complex problem of Italian infringement in EU environmental legislation is that of waste management. The number of open infringement proceedings regarding landfills is in some ways similar to that relating to infringements of EU legislation on urban waste water, an area related to the same "family" since it is connected to the poor governance of the territory; however, infringements regarding water seem to be relatively less severe. In fact, in the case of waste, Italy received a letter of formal notice in accordance with Article 260 TFEU, following the first ruling by the Court with reference to the emergency in Campania (Case C-297/08). It is also the only sector in which a sentence of a "general and persistent infringement" was given (Case C-135/05, with reference to the illegal dumping) and which affects the entire country.

It is clearly an issue in which regional powers are interlinked with the responsibilities of local authorities, whose management problems and solutions affect financial issues, related to the need for huge public investment in the reclamation and construction of disposal facilities. From this point of view, the possible application of financial penalties would only aggravate the problem by taking away further financial resources from the state budget resources which should be used for environmental policy.

As can be seen, the existence of national legislation that correctly implements European requirements on a formal level does not prevent the infringement of EU law. However, it is not possible to reconstruct this case as a mere infringement of application of the law since the structural situation is so severe and so widespread that it is clearly the result of a poor land management policy whose responsibility clearly lies with all levels of government and numerous decision makers.

Ultimately, the issue of waste shows a structural distance in Italian politics linked primarily to landfill and European politics which aims to transform waste from being a cost to becoming an economic resource to be exploited. The statements of Environment Commissioner Potočnik, released on 13 January 2012 on the occasion of the publication of a Commission study on the economic and employment benefits of a full implementation of EU waste legislation are particularly significant. According to the Commissioner:

> to bury that resource in the ground is worse than short-sighted. [. . .] waste management and recycling can make a big contribution to economic growth and job creation. If the existing legislation was implemented properly, we could avoid costly clean-up operations, pollution and health problems. And let's not forget that recycled materials are cheaper than virgin ones – and that they reduce greenhouse gas emissions and our dependence on imports.[18]

### *8.7.2 Hunting*

The infringements in the hunting sector are an example of serious non-compliance determined by regional legislation. More precisely, the infringements relate to the correct implementation of the "Birds" and "Habitats" directive and the way in which the regions implement the exemptions allowed by those directives. There are several cases in advanced stages in this sector (three of which have already received a letter of formal notice

18 See Press Release of the European Commission, 13 January 2012.

in accordance with Art. 260 TFEU) and this would seem to be a common problem on a national scale to the point that the Commission has reported a widespread misapplication of Article 9 of the "Birds" directive relating to the hunting exception which is only permitted in "small numbers" or for specific reasons.

The backdrop to this is well known: the Court of Justice has repeatedly ruled against the Italian state regarding various regional laws that are in conflict with EU law. Subsequently, the regions concerned have amended their legislation correctly transposing the "Birds" Directive on a formal level but still continue to grant exemptions for hunting which, according to the Commission, are in breach of Article 9. The Court also found a number of shortcomings of a general nature: for example, the Italian Government has adapted its legislation whereby the state has the power to cancel regional exemption measures even though this has never actually been applied.

During the litigation, the discussion between the state and the Commission is currently focusing on the interpretation of Article 9 which among other things permits exemptions within the limits of "small numbers" (Art. 9(1), letter C), a vague clause that allows the unlimited use of discretionary powers. A second line of work is being carried out at a political level: in 2009 the regions along with the Ministry of the Environment, submitted a request for the review of the Annex to the Directive on huntable species in Italy, which was later rejected by the Commission for non-recognition of the conservation status of the species. A second time, the regions, together with the Ministry of Environment and the Ministry of Agricultural Policies, agreed to ask for a review of the annex to the directive that would allow the hunting of starlings with a request being formally submitted to the European Commissioner on 8 July 2011. This time it was accompanied by a report from ISPRA stating that Italy is the only Member State, including those bordering the Mediterranean, where the hunting of this species is not allowed despite the favourable conservation state. In reference to this event, a lack of coordination between the ascending and the descending phase can be seen. In 2009 in fact, when the problem of infringements in Italy was widely known, a new directive on the conservation of wild birds (2009/147/EC) was adopted; Italy could have attempted a renegotiation of the content of the EU requirements, but there is no trace of this in the official documents of the Council.[19]

### 8.7.3 *The Waters*

Procedure 2007-4680 is an interesting case of incorrect implementation in which the failure to comply with Part III of Decree 152/2006 Directive 2000/60/EC establishing a

19 See Pres/2009/347 and minutes of the 2978th meeting of the Education and Youth Council, 26 and 27 November 2009.

framework for Community action in the field of water and for which the Italian state is currently in violation pursuant to Article 258 TFEU.

In relation to cases of incorrect implementation such as this, it can be seen that the Commission promptly contests non-compliance to the point that it will request the introduction of specific words in place of others in national legislation even if this wording is not decisive for the substance of the legislation.

At least in the cases of extremely detailed technical guidelines, the Commission itself seems to require a sort of photocopiable-fulfilment from the State, which on the one hand limits the discretion that "on paper" at least should be left to the States, and on the other hand, takes responsibility away from any state that has an interest in slavishly accepting requests made by the Commission, referring the management of the implementation problems to the application stage of the law.

With reference to the case mentioned, the Italian state, in reference to the observations made by the Commission, notes that the requirements were implemented through the use of various legislative tools and some complaints seem to stem from a disjointed reading of these instruments.

In other cases, the findings arise from a lack of contextualization of EU legislation on a national level in which on account of both the territorial needs and the linguistic adaptation in the terminology used within the directive, an adjustment was required during transposition.

A general practice that seems to go in this direction is the Commission's request included in the legislative proposal, that Member States put together correlation tables to link the transposition of internal measures they have taken for the directive and submit these to the Commission when they inform them of the transposition. It is not surprising that sometimes the mandatory provisions on correlation tables included in the proposed directives are suppressed by the Council during the legislative process.

### *8.7.4 Air Quality*

Another important element to be considered is that in some cases where there is an alleged infringement in Italy, this may also be lodged at a large number of other Member States.[20] This is the reason why it is plausible that common cause can sometimes generate the problem which may reside in the high level of ambition of the European environmental protection which makes the law difficult to enforce, or problems that affect the genetic moment of the supranational legislation or in its editorial quality.

In this regard, some useful indications are based on the documents relating to PM10, concerning the infringement of Directive 30/1999 (subsequently replaced by Directive 50/2008) and the subject of Case C-68/2011, currently pending Article 258 TFEU.

20 See Working Paper attached to the Annual Report on monitoring the application of Community Law (2010), SEC(2011) 1093 final, pp. 166 *et seq.*

In relation to European standards in the field of air quality and the exceedance of limit values of concentration of fine particles known as PM10, nearly all Member States have submitted requests for exemption (18 countries) and/or have been subjected to infringement proceedings (10 countries), some of which have already ended with a negative ruling (see Cases C-479/10 and C-365/10, relating to Sweden and Slovenia).
There are only four countries which are immune from formal complaints: Iceland and Luxembourg have not recorded limits in excess of the threshold; Finland and Lithuania have obtained permission from the Commission to exceed the limit values allowed by the Directive on seasonal pollution produced by some sources (*e.g.* road-sanding winter).
In the defence brief opposing the Commissions referral, Italy noted the lack of effective integration of EU policies on air quality and other policies such as climate and denounced the inconsistency of the measures required by the EU in different sectoral areas. For example, the European policies that aim to limit fuel consumption in the transport sector could facilitate the use of vehicles with a greater polluting potential and which are harmful to air quality. The same negative effect could be produced with reference to the spread of biomass production plants, sponsored by the EU in energy policy. In the coordination meeting in April 2011, Italy, while reiterating its commitment to continue strengthening measures to return to the limit values, suggested revising the directive, taking into account the specific characteristics of certain geographic areas, such as the Po valley.
While it is not possible to conduct a comparative systematic study, in several cases where the infringement is common to a number of states, the states themselves agree to put pressure on the Commission to "lower" EU legislation, a policy that Brussels has been inclined to postpone until all procedures for requests for exemption have been completed.
With reference to the case PM10 when Directive 2008/50/EC was adopted which reviewed the entire European regulatory framework on air quality, the agreement was reached in the Council by means of a compromise package which included various elements: if value limits are maintained at a certain level while taking into account the generalized difficulties in achieving air quality objectives, there is the possibility for states to obtain extensions in terms of fulfilment and flexibility.[21]

### 8.7.5 *Plastic Bags*

An interesting case which is currently under scrutiny by the Commission is that of plastic bags. In 2006, within the financial budget, Italy implemented a general ban on the marketing of non-biodegradable plastic bags from 1 January 2010. The application of this ban was subsequently postponed.

21 See the minutes of the 2740th session of the Environment Council, 27 June 2006 and PRES/06/192.

This legislation led to two proceedings. The first is an infringement proceeding concerning the breach of the notification of the ban on plastic bags (2011-4030). Following a number of complaints and requests from the plastics industry, the Commission argued that the Italian measure falls within the definition of "technical regulation" under Article 1, para. 11 of Directive 98/34/EC and in the definition of "measures" pursuant to Article 16 of the Directive on packaging: such measures must be notified to the Commission at the planning stage.

In this regard, there was also an intervention by the United Kingdom, which filed a detailed opinion, complaining that the benefits from this measure would be reaped by the Italian agricultural sector and national producers of bio-shoppers. It essentially complains that discrimination in favour of Italian industry is in breach of Article 34 TFEU, since the reasons given by Italy in relation to the measure do not justify the imposition of the marketing limitations: according to the United Kingdom there was no evidence of the proportionality of the measure compared to the objective pursued, thus allowing for a distortion the single market.

In the second proceeding which has not yet been formally opened against Italy (this is an EU-Pilot pre-infringement case), the Commission complains of the incorrect implementation of Article 18 of Directive 94/62/EC on packaging and packaging waste, as amended by Directive 2004/12/EC.

With a letter from the Minister of the Environment of 15 February 2011, Italy called upon the Commission to suspend all proceedings until the problem of the marketing ban on plastic bags was discussed in the Council of Ministers. This was because the Commission was considering the adoption of a proposal regulating the matter, as witnessed by the public consultation, launched on the internet in summer 2011, on the best way to reduce the use of bags: the measures in question included the bags being subjected to a tax, the introduction of a general ban on marketing in the EU and a tightening of the biodegradability requirements for packaging. A similar review request was also formally made by Italy.[22]

Even in light of the timing of the adoption of EU legislation, it is likely however, that the Commission will block the request to suspend the application of the ban.[23]

## 8.8 Concluding Remarks

In conclusion, it is clear that the basic causes of the non-compliance do not reside in the systemic adjustment tools of the internal Italian implementation system which, in the light of available data, have proven to be substantially efficient.

22 See Press Release of 3075th Environment Council: "Austria, supported by a large number of Member States asked the Commission to consider regulatory measures against the use of plastic bags".

23 *See* Art. 2 of Decree-Law 2/2012 "On urgent measures on environmental matters", in the course of conversion which suspends the marketing ban with respect to certain categories of bags.

The administrative management of disputes initiated by Brussels has also proven to be efficient and filters the cases whose criticality can be adduced to the lack of genuine commitment of the decision-makers involved, in fact cases which can be resolved, albeit with a delay which should be avoided,[24] when financial penalties are threatened, to the few serious cases in which the adjustment problems are structural and drown in the gap between the European policy in a particular field and the actual choices carried out by the state through its public powers, in an inextricable network of co-responsibility. The examples are those of waste management, but also hunting, the solution to which is simple if Italy did not continue to allow the hunting of species which are banned under EU law. The fundamental problems therefore do not seem to be a problem of rules, but of political will; therefore the remedies should be sought on this level.

With regard to the rules however, it is evident that the changes introduced by the Lisbon Treaty have strengthened the system for monitoring compliance with EU law by the Member States, both in its efficiency in terms of time and in its capacity to impose penalties, and this must be taken into account in the systematic plan, preventing the initiation of infringement proceedings for failure to transpose.

The variation of the terms of the delegations with the Finance Act 2012 seems to be a useful stopgap until a more comprehensive reform of the adjustment mechanisms allowing for the update of amendments to the treaties comes into force.

It should be mentioned that a bill to reform the Law 11/2005 was approved by the Council of Ministers in 2010. This would be a new system law which would regulate relations between Italy and the EU first of all for better coordination between the so-called ascending phase which is to be simplified and reorganized, and the so-called descending phase thus acting on the most critical profile of the current system of adapting the national system to EU law although the operating deficits of the ascending phase are not just a question of organization but are typical Italian problem with deep cultural roots.

It is clearly not possible to describe in detail here the innovations that relate to the instruments of adjustment. It is only possible to touch on the modification which during the annual Union law would entail two distinct measures: 1) European legislative delegation which includes exclusively legislative delegations and authorizations in the implementation through regulatory; and 2) European law containing provisions for direct implementation. This "doubling up" would allow the Government to have the legislative delegation necessary for transposition within a short and specified time period so as to be able to cope with accelerated infringement proceedings.

24 Out of a total of 549 infringement proceedings (up to November 2011) to be opened over the years and, as seen, for the most part subsequently closed, Italy has received one financial penalty.

## References

R. Adam & A. Tizzano, *Lineamenti di diritto dell'Unione europea* (2nd edn), Torino, 2010.

F. Astone, *Il processo normativo dell'Unione europea e le procedure nazionali per l'esecuzione degli obblighi comunitari*, Giappichelli, 2007.

B.A. Biejen, 'The Implementation of European Enviromental Directives: Are Problems Caused by the Quality of directives?', *European Energy an Enviromental Law Review*, 2011, pp. 150-163.

R. Bin & P. Caretti, *Profili costituzionali dell'Unione europea*, Il Mulino, 2009.

M. Cartabia & L. Violini, 'Le norme generali sulla partecipazione dell'Italia al processo normativo dell'Unione Europea e sulle procedure di esecuzione degli obblighi comunitari. Commento alla legge 4 febbraio 2005, n. 11', *Le Regioni*, 2005, pp. 475-512.

A. Celotto & G. Pistorio, 'Diciotto anni di "legge comunitaria"', in P. Caretti (Ed.), *Osservatorio sulle fonti 2006: le fonti statali: lo sviluppo di un decennio*, Giappichelli, 2007.

S. Baroncelli, *La partecipazione dell'Italia alla governancedell'Unione europea nella prospettiva del Trattato di Lisbona. Un'analisi delle fonti del diritto nell'ottica della fase ascendente e discendente*, Giappichelli, 2008.

S. Baroncelli (Ed.), *Il ruolo del Governo nella formazione e applicazione del diritto dell'Unione europea. Le peculiarità di un sistema costituzionale multilivello*, Giappichelli, 2008.

L. Daniele, *Diritto dell'Unione europea. Sistema istituzionale - Ordinamento - Tutela giurisdizionale - Competenze*, Giuffrè, 2010.

C. Fasone, 'Il Parlamento italiano dopo il Trattato di Lisbona, in vista dell'approvazione di una nuova legge sui rapporti con l'Unione europea', in *Studi parlamentari e di politica costituzionale*, 2010.

K. Lenaerts & J.A. Gutierrez-Fons, 'The General System of EU Environmental Law Enforcement', in *Yearbook of European Law*, 2011.

A. Singhofen & T. Lehtonen,'Parlamento europeo 2004-2009: punti salienti dell'attività legislativa in materia di protezione della salute umana e dell'ambiente', *Rivista giuridica dell'ambiente*, 2009, pp. 827-834.

P. Wennerås, 'A New Dawn for Commission Enforcement under Articles 226 and 228 EC: General and Persistent (GAP) Infringements, Lump Sums and Penalty Payments', *Common Market Law Review*, 2006, pp. 31-62.

P. Wennerås, *The Enforcement of EC Environmental Law*, Oxford University Press, 2007.